"Dealing with the pluralism and diversity in the modern Catholic parish can be a rather hectic experience. Greg Dues, combining sociology and theology, reflects on the parish and its people in transition. With an eye on history, he helps today's Catholic find his or her identity in a rapidly changing Catholic culture. His application of Vatican II's "hierarchy of truths" to the actual parish situation is a fine example of pastoral theology in action. His Case Studies, often humorous, always realistic, will be especially helpful to pastoral ministers, parish councils, and parish volunteers. Practical, sensitive, and pastoral, *Dealing with Diversity* fills a real need in today's church. I recommend it highly."

William J. Rademacher, Ph.D.
Director, Pastoral Ministry Program
Duquesne University
Author of The New Practical Guide for Parish Councils

DEALING

WITH

DIVERSITY

a guide for parish leaders

Greg Dues

TWENTY-THIRD PUBLICATIONS
Mystic, Connecticut

Twenty-Third Publications
P.O. Box 180
Mystic CT 09355
(203) 536-2611

ISBN 0-89622-256-6
Library of Congress Catalog Card Number 87-51565

Edited by John G. van Bemmel
Cover design by Jeff McCall
Interior design by William Baker

Acknowledgment
The letter on pages 99-100) by Bishop Kenneth J. Povish,
which originally appeared in the *Lansing Catholic Weekly*,
iis reprinted with the kind permission of the bishop.

CONTENTS

INTRODUCTION

Old, abandoned houses fascinate me, especially those in rural areas. Sometimes all that remain are foundation stones and some parts of walls. Even if these have disappeared, there remains evidence of a house of long ago: an evergreen tree deliberately planted and now standing as a lonely sentinel out of step with trees on the horizon, drooping lilac bushes now just wood, and perhaps some fruit trees long barren but once part of an orchard. These are not sad scenes for me because they remind me of a deeper reality. I feel the generations of life that once filled those homes and the excitement of new beginnings and the ever-repeating cycle of promise: weddings, love-making, births, childhood games, sickness, deaths, success, and failure. I feel an identity between the house and the people who had lived there. Now, long abandoned by descendants of people who knew it as home, the house is *walked past*. Eventually, my fascination with abandoned houses jelled into these lines, entitled "Any House," composed twenty-five years ago:

> Built, conceived in, cried in, fear-filled,
> Stands, laughed in, played in, love-thrilled,
> Fades, grown-old-in, memory-fast,
> Falls, died in, walked past.

This verse often speaks to me in these years following Vatican II. Used in numerous workshops and talks, it becomes the inspiration for this book. It speaks to me about historical transitions in the church and the passing of religious identities as people go about living church in a particular era. It speaks to me of the birth, life cycle, and destiny of "church" as people experience it.

This verse helps me and others to understand why parishioners feel threatened and why they agonize over the passing of their "church." Within that church they were conceived. In the faithful practice of their religion they sometimes experi-

1

enced fear and even tears. Yet it was a church of security, a religion that brought laughter and love. Like their ancestors before them, people expected to grow old in this church, clutching to themselves the memories of all that had made so much sense. Then it seems that almost overnight their children, friends, and even, they suspected, the church itself abandoned the beliefs and practices that had given them so much meaning. Their comfortable church "fell" and was "walked past" by those almost in a hurry to build a new church.

"Any House" also helps me to understand why new religious movements evolve within the church and why new and popular religious traditions and identities gradually replace the old. The cycle, ever present in the Catholic church, must and will go on.

Finally, "Any House" becomes an invitation to humility. The new religious viewpoints and efforts to which we devote ministerial energy will one day, too, be "walked past"!

This book is not about the tensions widespread in the national and international church. It is about those in the *local parish*. Part One puts this situation into context. It discusses the nature of pluralism, the tension in faith between theory and practice resulting in a plurality of religious viewpoints and practices as the norm in the history of the church, the connection between a loss of a Catholic identity and this new pluralism, and the question of sectarian features. Part Two offers some suggestions on how to minister in the midst of this pluralism. Part Three presents a series of situations that challenge the parish team in a fictitious parish. These situations are a small sample of the widespread diversity of religious thinking, lobbying, and practice in Catholic parishes a generation after Vatican II, the kind that causes stress and conflict for parish ministers and other leaders. A methodology is developed that uses these situations to challenge parish teams, parish leaders, volunteer workers, and other adult parishioners to work toward an experience of unity allowing for different religious identities, viewpoints, and practices.

PART ONE

THE CONTEXT
OF TODAY'S PLURALISM

1

THE SITUATION TODAY

Dozens of different religious convictions and practices compete for attention and acceptance in the contemporary Catholic parish. These do not concern fundamental matters of Christian faith such as trinity, divinity of Christ, and real presence in the eucharist. They concern, rather, practical expression of personal beliefs. Enthusiastic charismatics liberally practice the gifts of the Spirit to the consternation of more moderate parishioners suspicious of an emotional faith. Parishioners dedicated to questions of peace and justice challenge civil law and political policy while others write letters to the editor against these parishioners. Conservative abortion foes clash with parishioners promoting a more comprehensive respect for life agenda. Building committees making plans for church renovations face the ire of groups wishing to preserve the past. Parishioners, remembering the traditions of their youth, insist on black vestments and Latin prayers for funerals.

Probably no Catholic parish has a catalogue of all the different religious viewpoints, convictions, and practices within its congregation. No parish has them all, nor is any parish free of at least a little bit of variety. Some of this variety is very innocent and private. Some is very vocal, organized, and conflict producing. The following list, not meant to be exhaustive, points to a new phenomenon facing parish ministers:

Charismatics in firm union with Catholic tradition
Charismatics with an ecumenical flavor
Charismatics with close ties to Protestant Pentecostalism
Catholic fundamentalists
Catholic traditionalists organized around specific objectives (e.g. Catholics United for the Faith: C.U.F.) but remaining in union with the local church
Catholic traditionalists organized around rejection of Vatican II and a banned liturgy (Tridentine Catholics) Catholic traditionalists cooperating with the local parish but maintaining a pre-Vatican II spirituality
Pro-life groups who limit efforts to the abortion issue
Comprehensive pro-life groups
Peace and justice groups
Those who vocally oppose peace and justice groups and/or the philosophy of civil disobedience
Women's rights groups (within society at large with voices in the local parish)
Women's rights groups (regarding church ministries)
Those who oppose the philosophy and objectives of women's rights
Blue Army
Bayside devotees
Marriage Encounter
Renew groups
Gay/Lesbian groups

Such a diversity has created trying moments in the recent history of the Catholic parish. For generations traditional Catholic identity provided a sense of unity and the context for parishioners' faith. This identity has not survived the past twenty years of renewal, reform, and change within the church and within the societies in which the church lives. Now parishioners of all ages are "all over the ball park."

Ministering within this situation, besides pastors, are parish workers unheard of in the era before Vatican II: DREs, CREs, youth ministers, liturgists, pastoral ministers, and lay administrators of priestless parishes. Opportunities for special formation and graduate studies have introduced them to new ways of understanding the mysteries of religion, new ways of talking about them, and new ways of celebrating them. The result is, as often as not, a situation in which parish staff members and other parish leaders are not always in the same ball park as many of the parishioners.

Behavioral aspects of faith are very personal matters. Ever since early Christianity there has been official teaching, along with norms for acceptance of this teaching and guidelines for religious activity. What people actually believe, however, and how they live their belief are not only personal but often biased. In line with their personal beliefs and biases, parishioners also have precise notions of what they want the parish and the next generation to believe and how they want them to live religiously. This claim to know what the church does teach or should teach often causes conflict and stress situations for church personnel. It is a rare week when parish ministers do not feel the pinch of being caught between "the devil and the deep blue sea." Frequent turnover of lay parish personnel indicates that many are opting for the "deep blue sea" but finding that the "devil" can swim.

PLURALITY OF FUNCTIONING RELIGIOUS IDENTITIES

A new plurality of functioning religious identities lies at the heart of the stress and conflict within Catholic parishes today. The term "religious identity" describes how persons know themselves and their world in the context of faith. Adding "functioning" to "religious identity" distinguishes it from "theoretical" descriptions of who persons should be because they are Catholic parishioners in a particular era. A functioning religious identity describes who persons actually are as they live their faith. The term "functioning" therefore describes a behavioral and oftentimes intense dimension of a person's religious life. A religious identity provides the context in which a parishioners' faith, religious convictions, and religious practices hold together, make sense, and are expressed in word and action. It provides religious security.

A functioning religious identity is, in summary, the way people understand themselves religiously or are perceived by others regardless of their participation in and cooperation with the broader denominational or parish themes. One example of a functioning religious identity, but by no means the only one as the foregoing list indicates, is the charismatic phenomenon in Catholic parishes.

Parishioners representing these more intense functioning religious identities are preoccupied, sometimes in an exaggerated way, with a particular religious belief or grouping of beliefs and sometimes with a private interpretation of these beliefs. Individually or as groups, they rally around some particular aspect of Catholicism or what they insist should be Catholicism. For example, a charismatic might promote the release of the Spirit and speaking in tongues as part of ordinary parish life. Other parishioners may be preoccupied with and lobby for a promotion of the Bayside apparitions in the parish religious education programs. The Blue Army may insist that only the rosary is a legitimate peace endeavor whereas peace and justice groups may downplay the value of any parish activity that is not action oriented. In each of these cases, and dozens of others, there is a preoccupation with what is perceived or interpreted as important religious reality. This reality need not be defined by the official church. The church may not even approve of it, as in the case of Bayside.

Diversity of religious preoccupation may enrich the life and communion of the local parish or it may threaten it. If the preoccupation centers around beliefs ranking high in the church's hierarchy of truths and contemporary teaching, a positive pluralism can result. On the other hand, if the preoccupation centers around a belief that ranks very low in the hierarchy of truths, or a non-essential in Catholic tradition, or a private interpretation of religious reality, it may contribute to a tension within the parish and for the parish staff.

When "pluralism" is used in this book, it refers to the plurality of functioning religious identities as described above. It leaves much to be desired as do all "ism" words. Therefore, other descriptive phrases will frequently be used.

FORMS OF PLURALISM

The most obvious form of pluralism in the Catholic parish is the "clustering" kind. Religious preoccupation is accompanied by some aspects of organization: identification with each other in clusters, meetings, mutual support activities, some link to a broader group, regional or national conventions, and a tendency to lobby viewpoints privately with others or more publicly at parish meetings. Examples of clustering pluralism are charismatics, Catholics United for the Faith (C.U.F.), peace and justice groups, pro-life groups, women's rights groups, Catholic fundamentalists or traditionalists, some extreme Marian groups, Tridentine Catholics, etc. This kind of pluralism causes stress and potential conflict when it differs radically from a parish staff member's own functioning religious identity, when the lobbying becomes intense, when it contradicts broader theological themes promoted within the contemporary church, or when it leads to elitism or separatism within the parish community.

Another kind of pluralism happens when individual parishioners, not allied with any particular group, become preoccupied with a particular religious belief or private interpretation of religious reality often with a biased enthusiasm. Sometimes this preoccupation is the result of poor religious instruction or the affirming of parents' convictions and example. It may also be the result of a particular personal crisis. This kind of pluralism causes stress and potential conflict when these parishioners vocally reject current parish policies, for example, the use of lay eucharistic ministers and lectors, or when they vocally insist on practices the parish has down-played or cancelled in the process of renewal, for example, some traditions relating to first communion, first reconciliation, confirmation, and weddings. Often such stress areas come from a failure to distinguish between essentials and non-essentials within our religious tradition. Because religious identities, like traditions, are handed down, the functioning faith of the next generation is affected if parents or individual parish leaders such as catechists fall into this category.

LOSS OF CATHOLIC IDENTITY

Nostalgic Catholic parishioners, who are old enough to remember the pre-Vatican II church and parish, often refer to the time when everyone knew what it meant to be Catholic. Even their Protestant neighbors and friends knew what a Catholic did and believed. Now such parishioners use expressions that describe in lay terms the diversity of religious viewpoints and practices that have changed this traditional feeling within the Catholic parish: "No one knows what to believe any more. Now you can be a Catholic and do whatever you want." Between the mid-1960s and the mid-1980s Catholic parishioners lost much of their common pool of religious stories, symbols, and ceremonies, along with their clear-cut value system and their distinctive way of looking at their world.[1] This relationship between the loss of a Catholic identity and today's pluralism will be developed in Chapter 3.

STRESS AND CONFLICT

This loss of a Catholic identity was accompanied by the loss of an innocent variety of religious practices that was, so to speak, natural to parishioners before 1960. Protected by a common religious meaning shared by Catholics this pluralism did not cause stress and conflict within the parish. Competing religious convictions experienced in Catholic parishes today, however, differ from the diversity of the pre-Vatican II era in aggression, anger, stress, and conflict within the parish community. Parish ministers responsible for coordinating the practical faith of the community are often on the receiving end of these negative emotions. The old saying, "What you don't know won't hurt you," is seldom true today because these parish ministers usually know—and it does hurt.

It is easier and surely less traumatic, although not as interesting, to minister when all parishioners are united in religious beliefs and behavior. It is easier to minister to those of like mind and heart with oneself and to ignore or, worse, to fight those with differing convictions and behaviors. And fights there are. It is not unusual for a sour attitude to invade the parish with private wars, bitter arguments, and labeling of factions.

Before Vatican II there were no specialized parish workers as we know them today. Beginning with directors of religious education, they began to appear on the scene in the late 1960s. Soon DREs, liturgists, pastoral ministers, and specialists such as Christian service ministers became familiar on the parish scene. Ordinarily they possess post-Vatican II credentials. It is not unusual for such parish leaders to be committed to religious convictions and practices that differ theologically and behaviorally from those of parishioners and even pastors. Because specialized personnel often are under contract they are subject to evaluation and dismissal. If their functioning religious identity or the identity they promote does not match that of a pastor or a power-holding group, stress and eventual dismissal may result.

Conflict with Parents The handing on of religious traditions and the religious identity that holds these religious convictions together is a very personal and important matter for parents. Many parents want the parish to "make" their children to be like themselves. Their resentment might, therefore, be understandable when a religious educator promotes a change, at least in emphasis, in religious beliefs and practices contrary to their own religious viewpoints. Such a change might be taken as a personal affront to parents' convictions, for example, regarding details surrounding first communion, reconciliation, and confirmation. The same kind of resentment may occur when the religious educator changes the curriculum to conform to current theological themes or when the Christian service minister promotes peace and justice themes politically unpopular with some parishioners. The resulting aggression or lack of cooperation causes stress for the parish staff trying to be faithful to the changing times and to their own faith convictions. It is not unusual for a particular parish leader to resign or to be dismissed if this situation of conflict is not resolved.

Conflict with Catechists Catechists' personal religious identity, just as that of parents, presents possibilities of stress or conflict for a catechetical administrator coordinating religious education programs. They are in an immediate situation of influencing the religious identity of those in formation because their efforts are organized and on a regular basis. They are usually selected because of their obvious faithfulness to the church. However, this faithfulness may hide many religious biases. The commission to teach may provide the opportunity to hand on these biases and therefore contribute to further confusion in the parish. Administrators may find it difficult to remove the commission to teach from such catechists because they are volunteers. Moreover, because it is the responsibility of the religious educator to select, to train, and to evaluate catechists, a conflict of religious viewpoints may destroy what should be a good spirit within a parish ministry.

Conflict with the Pastor The loss of a shared religious meaning and identity sometimes occurs among parish team members themselves. Not rarely a pastor with traditionalist tendencies is assigned to a parish that has experienced years of progressive changes and ministries. The consequence is tension when the pastor ministers with team members from a previous administration among the same people, but from differing and sometimes contradictory religious priorities and convictions. Sometimes such a pastor is simply not comfortable with the team concept. Or such a pastor might be threatened by forms of ministry founded on theologies he is not comfortable or acquainted with. Because the pastor by tradition and Canon Law is still responsible for the overall administration of the parish, this stress situation often results in the dismissal of the more progressive staff members, regardless of support for them among the parishioners.

PLURALISM AND THE FUTURE

Andrew Greeley once projected that within a decade Catholics would not care any more about, among other things, the many movements that produce different functioning religious identities in the parish.[2] Now, ten years later, religious pluralism has increased and the accompanying stress and conflict indicate that parishioners do care. Furthermore, there is every reason to expect that in the future there will be even greater diversity within the Catholic parish than there is today. Analyzing the situation of the church in Germany fifteen years ago, Karl Rahner described what is also the American experience of a transition from a homogeneity to heterogeneity. He indicated that this change is related to the transitions occurring in the world around us.[3] Because these transitions are still in process, we can expect even greater diversity of religious viewpoints and practices in the future.

The right to make one's own religious choices is part of modern consciousness influencing religions. People today are neither driven by fate nor submissive to higher authority. This phenomenon, called the "heretical imperative,"[4] points to an even greater pluralism in parishes in the future. These insights will be explored more at length in Chapters 2 and 3.

PLURALISM AND POLARIZATION

There is always danger of polarization when pluralism is prevalent. This danger has become the experience of parish after parish. A diversity of religious viewpoints has been a healthy phenomenon in the church in the past and can be so again. Polarization, on the other hand, is always spiritually unhealthy, damaging to church community, and even sinful. Polarization does not occur just because there are many ways of believing and practicing one's faith in the parish. It happens when groups with differing opinions or expressions of faith no longer cooperate with each other for the good of the community, nor pray and worship with each other with good will. It happens when competing power groups evolve around religious issues with authority, sometimes presumed, claimed by one or the other. It happens when parishioners face repercussions of factionalism: either belong to a certain group or be shunned. Karl Rahner gives an excellent summary of the causes of polarization:

But the danger of a stupid and ultimately unfruitful polarization arises from other causes. People are thoughtless and suspicious of each other; they label each other "reactionary" or "progressive"; they attack each other, not with relevant arguments, but with outbursts of feeling. Each group, each periodical, each newspaper, is simply given whole-hearted approval or wholesale condemnation. Someone who holds a different opinion is at once assumed by the other to be stupid or wicked, to be reactionary or a modernist out to destroy Christianity. There are those who move only in circles which they feel instinctively to be sympathetic, without first examining them in a critical spirit. What is new is always accepted promptly by some as the last word of supreme wisdom and rejected by others as the greatest danger to Christianity of all times.[5]

THE CHALLENGE FOR PARISH MINISTRY

The Catholic parish can experience community while simultaneously experiencing pluralism. A sense of parish community is determined, not by a consensus of a particular "ideological position," but by the ability of parishioners to interact with positive feelings toward each other.[6] To minister effectively within a contemporary Catholic parish, therefore, parish leaders should be qualified to coordinate a diversity of religious convictions and practices into a positive experience for the local church community. Promotion of a unity within diversity, however, is not an admission that all divergent viewpoints and practices are good for the parish. Some lead to separatism or elitism; others are so far on the fringe of Catholic experience that their defenders' communion with the parish and therefore with the Catholic church might be questioned. Still others are founded on religious convictions that are self-induced or completely nonessential within true Catholic tradition.

To meet the challenge it is important that parish leaders 1) understand the causes of pluralism, 2) possess a clear, mature, theologically sound religious identity that holds together their own spirituality and motive for ministry, 3) possess a sound appreciation of the church's contemporary catechesis and an understanding of the difference between essentials and non-essentials in Catholic religious tradition, 4) possess an insight into the many functioning religious identities that are multiplying in the parish and exercise an openness to whatever benefits the parish community, and 5) possess the skills to help parishioners discover a shared religious meaning, a Catholic identity, which will help parishioners celebrate a unity in the midst of diversity.

SUMMARY

Parishioners today live their faith in a great variety of ways. As individuals or organized groups they rally around certain religious beliefs or cluster of beliefs from the church's body of teaching and traditions or from what they perceive and interpret as the church's teaching and tradition. Whether or not this pluralism contributes positively or negatively to the life of the parish depends on how this variety fits into the contemporary catechesis of the church—or does not fit. Today's pluralism differs from the diversity before Vatican II in its aggression and in the stress or conflict it causes the parish ministers. The loss of a shared religious meaning or Catholic identity within the Catholic parish lies at the heart of today's pluralism. This pluralism will very likely increase in coming generations. Parish team members play an important role in a revival of unity within diversity. It is important that they possess a theologically sound personal religious identity, an openness to other religious identities, skill in ministering within pluralism and, ideally, some skill in coordinating differing functional religious identities within one believing community.

2

PRACTICE AND THEORY

Religious pluralism is based on a very simple premise: religious reality for one person is not necessarily the same for another even in a single church community. People relate to sacred mysteries in at least slightly different ways. One's own religious or moral convictions do not always match those of another believer.

Religious pluralism has not always been officially tolerated within society at large and especially within religious communities. Yet it always existed. Even when religious pluralism is considered a sign of health in society at large, as it is in North America, it still creates agony within a religious community because of a longstanding conviction that God has confided absolute truth to its believers.

A diversity of religious viewpoints has always been characteristic of the Catholic community, even during those long eras when church leadership did not want to admit it or to tolerate it.

PRACTICE VERSUS THEORY

Ever since Pentecost there has been a tension between how the church wants her baptized to live and how they actually understand and live their faith—a tension between theory and practice. Continuing reflection on the part of theologians, church leaders, and individual believers results in religious *theory*. In view of God's revelation what should the community of baptized be like? This reflection has resulted in distinct *theologies* over the centuries. A catechetical theology was prominent in the earliest generations of Christianity and is preserved in the New Testament. The Fathers of the Church developed an apologetical theology during the second and third centuries to defend and explain Christian beliefs. A theology based upon neo-Platonism and Roman juridical thought provided the basis for the great christological definitions of the early councils. A devotional theology arose within the monastic movement. Scholastic theology developed in the Middle Ages within the universities. It would evolve into what is known as "Thomism," the commonly used theology in the Western Catholic church before Vatican II. New theologies continue to evolve today as illustrated by the emergence of process theology and liberation theology.

Theory also results in what are known as "models of the church." We can identify some of these already in the New Testament. The church is the "Kingdom of God" (the favorite model in the gospels), the "people of God" (I Peter 2:9-10), and "the body of Christ" (I Corinthians 12:12-30). Beginning in the Middle Ages and continuing into modern times, the church was considered "the perfect society," with emphasis on institutional and hierarchical aspects. This popular notion of the church was broadened and enriched by the *Dogmatic Constitution on the Church (Lumen Gentium)* of Vatican II, which returns to the model of "the people of God" with emphasis on the human and communal side of the church. Further insights were contributed by the publication of Avery Dulles's *Models of the Church*.[1]

Actual *practice* of faith challenges the bounds of theory as found in theology and models of the church. Practical faith evolves from immediate experience, charism of a preacher, influence of significant others, a particular emphasis—or bias—in faith formation, cultural factors, and the need of people to live religiously in practical and personal ways. Frequently this leads to a preoccupation with a particular religious reality or interpretation of religious reality with an intensely behavioral dimension: a functioning religious identity.

Because believers are very human, their practical faith is always much more human than are theologies and models of the church. Theologies have a sense of purity, exactness, and comprehensiveness about them. They are constructed with great care. Practical faith, on the other hand, is like those it serves: incomplete, limited, and historically bound. Human elements have a way of sneaking around the finest theory.

It is understandable, then, that practical faith is character- ized by a variety of practices not necessarily conforming to the- ory. This happens when individuals or groups attempt to speak of the unlimited mystery in ways not yet spoken, to live it in ways not yet lived, to emphasize it in ways not yet empha- sized. In doing so, some believers since the earliest Christian generations drifted from the core teachings of the church and became known as heretics. Others remained orthodox and their convictions and traditions were assumed into the broader iden- tity of what would become Catholicism. Examples of both are described in Chapter 3.

PLURALISM OF PRACTICE AS THE NORM

The New Testament (NT) gives indications of very di- verse views within Christianity as well as references to Christian groups regarded as radically deviant by NT writers. Sometimes the views are espoused by different groups coexisting within the same city as, for instance, the four affiliations described in I Corinthians 1:12 or the dis- pute at Antioch (Galatians 2:12-14). Sometimes one form of Christian outlook may have been prominent in one area and another in a different area, as we can deduce from comparing very different NT works that show no knowl- edge of each other. Nevertheless, the image of a totally homogeneous Christianity in the first Christian century is hard to erase.[2]

With these words alluding to pluralism in the first generation of Christianity, Raymond E. Brown and John P. Meier begin their book, *Antioch & Rome*. It is hard, they say, to erase the image of a totally homogeneous *first century* Christianity. It is hard to erase the image of a totally homogeneous nineteen cen- turies of church life for many if not most Catholics. How the church functioned in their youth or in the time of their immediate ancestors is often presumed to be the way the church functioned at the time of the apostles. Yet there has never been in the Catholic church *one* way of believing or *one* way of practicing what is believed. On the functioning level, no one particular expression of faith, of an individual or of an organized group, gives an adequate account of the significance, content, or motives for believing. Perhaps this is the best definition of "catholic": open to a variety of expressions of truth and therefore open to all religious identities functioning in communion with the church.

This historical variety of religious viewpoints and practice within the Catholic parish reflects the variety that is evident in all of creation and human life. Nothing could be more dull than a sameness throughout our environment and a total predictability within human life. And nothing could be more dull than a sameness throughout the Catholic church and a total predictability within religious faith.

Diversity of conviction and practice in the Catholic parish also reflects the richness and variety in sacred mysteries themselves. This diversity need not, therefore, be a threatening situation; competition and conflict need not rule the day. On the other hand, if freedom of divergent viewpoints and practices is automatically ruled out as a sin of disunity, division, or disloyalty, the practice of faith becomes narrow, rigid, and fundamentalistic. This does not mean that relativism—"everything is okay"—should be our goal. Conflict would be avoided but so would the values of healthy dialogue and confrontation.

A healthy family life can teach a powerful lesson about religious pluralism in the parish. Husband, wife, and children are stimulated to reach their individual potential and fulfillment both independently and in union with each other. There is diversity in such a family, and family in such a diversity.

Positive pluralism has always benefited the church. What the Extraordinary Synod of Bishops in Rome in 1985 said about the unity and pluriformity of particular churches within the universal Catholic church can be applied to the pluralism within the local parish:

When pluriformity is true richness and carries with it fullness, this is true catholicity. The pluralism of fundamentally opposed positions instead leads to dissolution, destruction, and the loss of identity.[3]

Archbishop Pio Laghi, the apostolic pronuncio to the U.S., echoed this theme with even stronger words while speaking to the U.S. bishops at their 1987 fall conference: "A plurality that cannot be integrated into unity is chaos; unity unrelated to plurality is tyranny."

It is a function of the parish and its leadership to make a plural expression of faith possible rather than impossible:

> In community we find our individual biases and convictions bounded by, complemented by, and challenged by others. This is both a threat and a gift. As a gift my community—indeed my religious tradition— fills out the narrowness of my own vision, welcomes my strengths and special insights, and makes up for my limitations. Pluralism, in this understanding, is an essential characteristic of a believing community, not to be apologized for, denied, or simply overcome, but to be invoked as a resource and strength. This is how faith flourishes in a group and carries individual belief beyond itself; this is how we are incorporated and our faith made communal.[4]

PLURALISM IN THE NEW TESTAMENT CHURCH

Pluralism of practice as a norm in the church was established almost before the winds and flames died down at Pentecost. The tendency of local churches, in the last third of the first century, was to go off in different directions as they lived their faith and to make sure that their faith would survive in spite of the death of the apostles.[5] Even while the apostles still lived there was evidence of pluralism. For example, there were four distinct functioning religious identities in the first generation church at Antioch. The first group insisted on full observance of the Mosaic Law, including circumcision; the second, the kosher food laws but not circumcision; the third did not insist on either circumcision or kosher food laws; the fourth did not insist on circumcision, kosher food laws, and also felt free from all aspects of Jewish cult and feasts. Three of these groups were associated with an apostle: James with the first group, Peter with the second, and Paul with the third. They had their problems with each other and eventually Paul had to leave. However, all these groups lived, worshipped, and grew in the Lord in one city at one time.

A reflection on the Acts of the Apostles gives some insights into how the church's leaders attempted to deal with this pluralism in ways that sound familiar today. First there is an attempt at a theoretical solution based on Peter's vision (Acts 10:9-16). Theoretically there is no difference between foods; all comes from God. However, sides continued to be drawn up between Christians who insisted on the observance of traditions inherited from their Hebrew background and Christians who insisted on the need to adjust to the freedom of non-Hebrew converts. Leadership wavered and Peter backslid into the camp of the traditionalists. Paul championed the progressive cause: freedom in Christ Jesus, freedom from old traditions for the sake of present and future missionary work among Gentiles. Those, on the other hand, who insisted on keeping the old traditions claimed that the non-observers could not be saved (Acts 15:1-2).

For the first of many times in her history, the church looked to a council of authority for a solution to internal conflict caused by pluralism (Acts 15:2-29). Chaired by the apostle James, the bishop of Jerusalem, the council listened first to Peter who had swung back to the progressive cause (Acts 15:7-11). Paul and Barnabas then testified to the assembly about the signs and wonders worked by God among the progressive Christians (Acts 15:13-29). James suggested a compromise which the council adopted and published for the whole church (Acts 15:13-29): all baptized were to observe the kosher law and traditional sexual code, but need not be circumcised.

This summary of one conflict among religious identities within the first generation of the church shows a sequence or stages still evident in the church community today as it wrestles with conflict caused by divergent viewpoints and practice both in the local parish and in the church at large:

1. Direct appeal to God's will by one or both parties or by someone in authority. "How can I be wrong if God is on my side?"
2. Private intervention on the part of church leaders in an attempt to defuse the conflict.
3. A breaking into factions championing one or the other side of the issue.
4. Development of theological arguments.
5. Intervention by the official church authority, e.g., by a council, pastoral letter, or decree.
6. Compromise.

This sequence toward solution did not end the matter for the early Christians, nor does it today ordinarily. Conflict continued and Paul, especially in his letter to the Galatians, continued to develop a theological foundation for the progressive cause. The conflict caused by this particular situation was finally resolved by history. As Christianity spread throughout the Roman Empire, the majority of those coming to baptism were people without previous Jewish traditions. In A.D. 70 Jerusalem was tragically destroyed by Roman armies. Jewish survivors scattered. The conservative Jewish Christian community eventually disappeared into history, separated from the rapidly growing Gentile Christian church.

This resolution of a particularly troublesome, stressful situation by the passing of time highlights the practical advice given by the Pharisee Gamaliel to the Sanhedrin. The advice is valid today and perhaps should be reflected on more often. In dealing with the followers of Jesus as an aspect of pluralism within the Jewish synagogue, he says (Acts 5:38-39):

Let them alone. If their purpose or activity is human in its origins, it will destroy itself. If, on the other hand, it

comes from God, you will not be able to destroy them without fighting God himself.

Among the many divergent religious practices evident in New
Testament times, there is one centered on the expectation of
Jesus' imminent return in glory. After a while this expectation
seems to have caused, among some of the baptized, a lack of interest in working. Paul, himself an advocate of this imminent
return, finally orders shunning those refusing to work (2 Thessa-
lonians 3: 6-15):

> In the name of the Lord Jesus Christ, we urge you, brothers,
> to keep away from any of the brothers who refuses to work
> or to live according to the tradition we passed on to you.

Still another clearly defined religious practice evident in the
letters of Paul is one that has had a revival in our own time,
namely, the charismatic phenomenon that seems to have been
popular in the city of Corinth. It was characterized by excitement in the believer of the Spirit's presence and by the release
of the Spirit in the gifts of prophecy, speaking in tongues, the
interpretation of this speaking, and healing. As church leadership still does today when necessary, Paul set down guidelines
to maintain unity within the local church in light of this particular expression of faith (I Corinthians 14:1-40).

These examples of religious pluralism in the first-generation
church, some with evident stress and conflict, have parallels in
every generation to the present day. In communities of believers
there is a mysterious mixture of the human and the divine. It is
natural that there be conflicting attitudes and convictions about
how religious truth and faith are to be humanly expressed. People will continue to claim the authority of God or Bible in support of their convictions. Others, especially in recent generations, may appeal to God-given human sciences such as
psychology and sociology. There will be statements and clarifications from authority. There will be councils, synods, pastoral
letters, compromises—and some heated arguments. There will

be writers adept at developing arguments for one or the other side. However, all can still enjoy the wonder of unity despite conflicting attitudes and opinions because a divine spirit of unity is present. For this unity Jesus prayed (John 15:11-12; 17-21):

> All this I tell you that my joy may be complete. This is my commandment: love one another as I have loved you....that all may be one as you, Father, are in me, and I in you; I pray that they may be one in us, that the world may believe that you sent me.

SUMMARY
There has always been a variety of religious viewpoints and practices in the church, which is to be expected as people go about living their faith. It is a consequence of the tension between theory and practice. Theory explains how the baptized should believe and live religiously; practical faith is how the baptized actually believe and live religiously. The first-generation church already gave evidence of this tension between theory and practice.

3

PLURALISM OF PRACTICE: THE NORM

Religious pluralism continued into all succeeding generations. Some divergent viewpoints and practices were assumed into Catholic beliefs and traditions and as such survived as part of a Catholic identity. Some of them are still present today; some disappeared with the passing of time. Others were declared heretical and continued in a separate communion. Still others were forcefully suppressed by execution of leaders and even by church-funded armies in the case of large groups. There were dozens of particular ways of being Christian or Catholic in each generation. Only some can be considered here.

HERETICAL PLURALISM

The last apostle was only recently dead when the first heresies were born. Heresy happens when a religious conviction and practice significantly distorts the church community's understanding of core religious beliefs. These early heresies are understandable because neither heresy nor orthodoxy was clearly distinguished at the beginning. There was no clearly defined and developed teaching nor a recognized hierarchy of religious truths. The church's great creeds, which would give an early structure to religious orthodoxy, had not yet been debated, written, and promulgated: the Nicean Creed from the Council of Nicea in 325 and its further clarification from the Council of Constantinople in 381. There were obvious differences of theological opinion even about Jesus the Christ, as the Johannine community gives evidence of, but no evident break in communion.[1]

This situation began to change at the turn of the first century when some groups in the church began to resist developments that were taking place in other groups. It was becoming obvious that there were contradictions among the different views held about such important mysteries as the nature and meaning of Christ. Only a century after the death and resurrection of Jesus, bishops began meeting in synods to decide which of the contradictory views were most faithful to the traditions of the apostles and which distorted them in a significant way. The question of orthodoxy and heresy was born.

Early heresies are usually recognized only by students of church history. Each of them, however, along with heresies throughout history, are examples of practical faith and functioning religious identities at a particular time and in a particular place. Gnosticism promoted a salvation through a special knowledge possessed only by the elite few. Adoptionism denied that Jesus is divine, and Docetism taught almost the opposite, namely that Jesus only appeared human. Manichaeism insisted that material things and therefore sexuality are evil and to be rejected. Manichaean tendencies appear under different forms repeatedly throughout church history.

In the mid-fourth century the Roman Empire and the church which was coextensive with it turned into a battleground between two ways of understanding and living the mystery of Jesus. The followers of the priest Arius rallied around an interpretation of the mystery of Jesus that denied his equality with God. Orthodox Catholics rallied around the doctrine of the trinity and the creed as proclaimed at the Council of Nicea. At one time the majority of Catholic bishops followed Arius. "Probably more Christians were slaughtered by Christians in these two years (342-343) than by all the persecutions of Christians by pagans in the history of Rome."[2] The success of Arianism was due in large part to the promotion of identity and solidarity among the invading "barbarian" Ostrogoths in relation to the old Roman establishment. This is an example of how cultural and political factors often influence the rise and fall of both heretical and orthodox religious convictions.

Heretical convictions and practice continued to thrive despite church councils. Apollinarianism, condemned at the First Council of Constantinople in 381, overemphasized the divinity of Jesus to the extent that he was left with no human soul. Nestorianism, condemned at the Council of Ephesus in 431, divided Jesus into two persons and claimed that Mary was the mother of the human person only. Monophysitism, condemned at the Council of Chalcedon in 451, argued that Christ's human nature was completely absorbed by the divine nature. Pelagianism promoted a doctrine of justification and grace that assumed that salvation is caused by human effort alone. Augustine led the fight against this heresy.

At no time in the history of the church has there been an absence of heretical religious convictions and practices. Among the estimated 150 heretical sects that plagued the church in the thirteenth century were the Cathari or Albigenses. Echoing the ancient heresy of Manicheanism, the Cathari preached that the material universe was the creation and tool of Satan, condemned the use of all material things, prohibited marriage, and sometimes encouraged suicide. There was a strong anticlerical streak in this and other heretical groups of that century due in large part to the scandalous activity of the clergy and temporal preoccupation of church leadership. A church sponsored crusade against the Cathari, one of the regrettable ways the official church of long ago dealt with divergent religious viewpoints, resulted in the massacre of men, women, and children, 20,000 in one city alone.[3] The experience of the official church with the Cathari resulted in the establishment of the sometimes notorious Inquisition, which for more than seven hundred years would keep a careful eye on what people believed. Often in its early history it stamped out with execution those who deviated from the conventional beliefs.

Not all movements away from traditional beliefs were declared heretical. Each generation had its examples of popular but questionable or heterodox religious convictions; for example, in the eighth century there was a wave of iconoclasm (destroying or abolishing all religious images) in the Eastern church. In the late 1700s, there was a movement (Febronianism) to restore the church to its primitive purity in the hope of affecting a complete reunion of all the Christian churches. It championed the divine right of bishops over against the pope, denying the separate infallibility of the latter. This movement was condemned at Vatican I in 1870.

BECOMING HERETICAL

The relation of heresy to pluralism is important because of frequent claims by individuals and groups that the "other" is heretical. Seldom does a single person or a group set out to be heretical. It is usually only in retrospect, after in-depth examination, that a particular religious conviction and practice is clearly understood and officially pronounced as heretical. Probably every believer unknowingly entertains "heretical" thoughts and speaks heresy in passing. As a pastor once quipped, "Every time I enter the pulpit I find myself a modalist" (condemned heresy that the one person of God has appeared under different forms, or modes, as Jesus and Spirit).

Three elements clearly define heresy: 1) a rallying around or promoting a particular interpretation of religious reality, but refusing to accept the whole body of the core teaching of the church, 2) a definite break with the recognized authority of the church community, and 3) a break with the local communion of the church.

Heresy in the truest sense, therefore, interprets the core of religious reality contrary to the way the church community understands and experiences it and the teaching church explains it. When many interpret religious reality in the same way, heresy solidifies into a movement and sometimes into a separate communion or church.

ORTHODOX PLURALISM

Divergent religious viewpoints and practices usually stay within the Catholic communion. It is this kind of pluralism that has provided a rich variety of religious traditions over nineteen centuries and can make the same contribution today. The evolution of an orthodox religious identity can be summarized in this way: An experience of religious reality or an emphasis on a particular aspect of religious belief becomes popular among believers *at a particular time and in a particular place*, sometimes under the influence of local church leaders and sometimes in spite of them. If this particular religious belief or emphasis survives, spreads to other communities, and is no threat to the core teachings of the church, it becomes a popular tradition and as such is handed on to succeeding generations. *These traditions are then assumed into what is known as "Catholicism" in any particular age.* Unlike heresies that are for us frozen in time and history by way of public condemnation, orthodox traditions sneak into the practice of Catholicism, so to speak.

As Christianity spread throughout the Empire, then throughout the European continent and finally to all corners of the earth, it received an even greater pluralistic character than it had during New Testament times. The culture and the biases of the different peoples produced different "brands" of orthodoxy. Superstitious practices and elements of pagan worship remained after "barbarian" tribes accepted conversion as they swept over the Roman Empire. Christianity in northern Africa, under Augustine the most thriving part of the church, differed from what would become Celtic Christianity in the British Isles. Irish Christianity had a monastic flavor. Its emphasis upon private penance for sin was spread throughout Europe by its missionary monks.

A generally poor quality of formation for religious leaders, primarily parish priests, resulted in religious ideas and practices far removed from the fundamentals of Christianity. The official church's frequent concern about temporal power rather than the gospel message resulted in a variety of religious practices that were centered in externals and in non-essentials. Time after time, great cultural shifts influenced the way people functioned religiously. A shared understanding of the church as the "perfect society" and as a powerful temporal institution managed to hold all together.

Some examples will clarify the pattern of how religious convictions and preoccupation with a particular religious reality becomes part of Catholic tradition.[4] During the time of Roman persecutions of Christians—off and on from A.D. 67 to 315—martyrdom provided an ideal means of total union with Christ's own death and resurrection. A cult surrounding these early martyrs became popular.[5] Christians visited their places of death and burial. Shrines and finally splendid basilicas were built over their tombs. Eventually, it became important that every parish church and finally every altar should be a martyr's shrine containing the relics of a martyr or saint. This policy was eventually mandated by church law. Feast days with lavish processions and devotions commemorating the birthday (day of death or martyrdom) of saints filled the church's calendar. The newly baptized assumed the name of a saint, and it became customary—still true today—to name the local parish church after some saint. This preoccupation with saints and sacred places entered the Catholic identity as one of the early non-scriptural religious traditions.

During the 300s, the church became an institution of millions of people free under Roman law. With this freedom came a tendency toward leniency and involvement in the "world." A minority of Christians, beginning in Egypt, chose to leave the "world" and its pleasures and to seek salvation in the desert through practices—often extreme—of bodily penance, chastity, and prayer. Eventually, some of these Christians banded together in community life. This movement, known as monasticism, spread to the West and under Benedict received a highly organized form, including the taking of public vows. Monasticism eventually became so influential that it affected the prayer life and attitudes of clergy and laity. To this day the custom of ringing the Angelus bell in parish churches imitates the monastic call to prayer. Monasticism continues into contemporary Catholicism only as an organized form of religious life, therefore excluding married laity. However, its original motivation of suspicion of evils rampant in the "world" has always been a subtle theme within Catholicism.

The loss of the core meaning of eucharist among the laity resulted in eucharistic devotionalism far removed from the original meaning of the memorial of the Lord's Supper. As the divinity of Christ and his presence in the eucharist became emphasized, people found it as important, if not more important, to look at and adore the holy bread than to take and eat it.

This new, static, and less traditional understanding of the eucharist was compounded by the ever-growing separation of clergy and laity. This separation reflected the social levels in the society the church found itself in, first the Roman Empire and eventually the feudal structures in Europe consequent to the conversion of the Germanic tribes. This separation was sealed by the canonization of Latin as the official language of worship and education during the Gregorian reform in the second half of the eleventh century. From that time Catholicism featured a popular eucharistic piety centered in adoration of the Blessed Sacrament, holy hours, Benediction, Corpus Christi processions, but infrequent communion.

A preoccupation with Mary, the Mother of Jesus, has probably produced a greater variety of religious traditions than any other aspect of Catholicism. Feast days in her honor began to multiply after the Council of Ephesus. As spirituality became more and more divorced from the Bible, Mary's perceived power of intercession and maternal influence over God became more popular and Christ's role more stern. The Middle Ages saw the development of those traditional doctrines concerning Mary that would eventually give Catholicism a strong Marian characteristic.

Marian spirituality continued to grow. "The Little Office of Our Lady" was prayed by religious and laity. The "Hail Mary" became one of the prayers all Catholics were expected to memorize and pray. Saturday was dedicated to Mary just as Sunday was to her son. Marian hymns and litanies multiplied during the eleventh and twelfth centuries. The rosary came into popular use early in the twelfth century as a substitute for the Book of Psalms. It had first consisted of 150 "Our Fathers" (a popular penance in the confessional) but under the influence of Dominic, founder of the Dominican Order (d. 1221), it had become 150 "Hail Marys." The "Angelus" also became popular: the recitation of Hail Marys and other prayers to Mary three times a day at the ringing of the church bells.

Marian spirituality reached possibly its extreme form under the influence of Louis de Montfort (d. 1716). He initiated the so-called true devotion to Mary, popularly known as slavery to Mary, requiring absolute surrender to Mary as mystics had surrendered themselves to Christ.

Visions of Mary and special revelations, popular already in the fourteenth century, increased as the centuries passed. Some of them received the official approval of the church, for example, Lourdes, Fatima, Guadalupe in Mexico, Knock in Ireland, Czestochowa in Poland, and Montserrat in Spain.

MAINTAINING ORTHODOXY
These examples of orthodox religious diversity show that pluralism has always been a feature of Catholicism and of the parish. Orthodoxy has nothing to do with popularity, but divergent orthodox viewpoints and practices have these characteristics: 1) they emphasize some aspect of religious belief not in contradiction with church's teaching although not always high in its hierarchy of truths; 2) proponents maintain union with the authority of the church community, and 3) function within and maintain contact with the broader local parish communion.

The following chapters deal with orthodox pluralism during the generations immediately prior to Vatican II and the new kind of pluralism today.

SUMMARY
When practical faith is founded on an interpretation of religious reality that significantly distorts the church's interpretation of its core teaching, a break in communion occurs and the practical faith becomes heresy. However, a particular empha-

sis, interpretation, or practice remains orthodox when communion with authority and the local community is maintained. It is this variety of faith practice that has given Catholicism its particular identity.

4

TRANSITION TO A NEW PLURALISM

Conventional religious practices[1] common in parishes before Vatican II need to be considered because of the radical difference between the two eras separated by this council, because today's pluralistic practice of faith is often either a deliberate rejection or defense of conventional Catholicism, and because pre-Vatican II conventional Catholicism gives a hint of how to deal with pluralism today.

CONVENTIONAL CATHOLICISM
Conventional Catholicism had these features:

1. A belief in a God who is everywhere but a dependence on the kind of prayer style and mental images that would seem to indicate that God is elsewhere, in a heaven separated from us and surrounded by angels and saints. This God, along with angels and saints, was depicted in human terms.
2. Emphasis on correct words, rituals, religious practices, devotions, blessed objects, and holy places as a means of coming into contact with divine presence, power, and effect.
3. A rich devotional life centered either in a non-scriptural dimension of Christ (e.g., the Sacred Heart and adoration of the Blessed Sacrament) or rallying around the power and mediation role of Mary and canonized saints.

4. Emphasis on exact observance of the church's law and discipline.

5. A tendency toward multiplication of religious activities and devotions rather than depth of religious experience.

6. A form of fundamentalism regarding Scripture and religious meaning.

7. A formation system that emphasized correct summary knowledge of doctrine, moral teaching, and religious practices.

8. A strong emphasis on the teaching authority of the church.

9. A sharp distinction between clergy and laity and a high dependency of the latter upon the former.

10. A tendency to judge the religious faith of a person by commitment to all of the above.

This conventional Catholicism is an example of a "plausibility structure" of religious worlds. A plausibility structure[2] is made up of a particular complex of religious ideas along with various practical and theoretical maintenance procedures that keep the ideas alive. Within a particular religious world, for example, the Catholic parish before Vatican II, people confirm for one another that their commonly held religious ideas are to be taken for granted as reality. In this plausibility structure authority figures are official "reality-definers." In the Catholic church these definers of religious reality theoretically were the local pastor, the bishop, the pope, and Vatican offices. In practice, the Baltimore Catechism defined the religious reality for the young people of the parish for the rest of their lives.

ROOTS OF PRE-VATICAN II CATHOLIC IDENTITY
Conventional Catholicism before the 1960s had its roots in history: centuries of accumulation of popular religious traditions and devotional spiritualities. These were emphasized in the practical life of the parish and in its formation system because the official Latin liturgy of the church was quite foreign to ordinary parishioners.

Also at the root of the pre-Vatican II religious identity, unknown to pastors and parishioners alike, was an essentialist understanding of Thomism. This theological approach developed an understanding of religious reality by way of definitions and analysis of concepts. Since the threatening Reformation movements of the 1500s, this approach had been canonized by the church throughout her practical formation system. It remained the foundation of the church's philosophy, theology, and self-understanding until the Vatican II era.

Characteristics of the essentialist approach are recognizable to anyone who received religious formation before Vatican II. Faith was presented and accepted without historical context. Little or no attention was paid to sociological, cultural, or psychological factors in either learning or living the faith. No need was felt to learn from the surrounding world because the church possessed all that was necessary for salvation. Stress was put on the cognitive rather than the experiential dimension of human learning. Studying doctrines, usually by way of definitions, was of primary importance. Finally, reality was neatly divided into the natural and the supernatural with emphasis upon the supernatural as *religious* truth.

This method of faith formation eventually produced a comfortable religious structure that all Catholics could relate to throughout the world. All men preparing for the priesthood were instructed from Latin manuals that were practically identical throughout the country, indeed throughout the world. They were ordained with a common message and points of emphasis for the people they would serve. The Baltimore Catechism, which became popular after its approval in 1885, was a practical summary of these seminary manuals. Most children were instructed from this catechism, usually by pastors and nuns, for almost a century. The resulting uniformity within the church was further strengthened by the policy of many dioceses to publish sermon outlines, often following the table of contents of the Baltimore Catechism. Finally, in communities heavily populated by Catholics there was little influence on or challenge to one's traditional religious practices from outside sources.

PLURALISM WITHIN THE PRE-VATICAN II
CONVENTIONAL IDENTITY

At first glance, Catholicism before Vatican II seemed to enjoy a sense of homogeneity. Many parishioners still harken to the "good old days" when there was security in the uniformity, or near sameness, among all Catholic parishes. In spite of this feeling of homogeneity, *pluralism in the pre-Vatican II era was very pronounced*. It was different, for the reasons developed below, in that it did not cause the stress and conflict within the parish that pluralism often does today.

When a Catholic wanted to rally around a particular cluster of religious truths or experiences, this could happen without tampering with the universal and secure conventional Catholic identity. In fact this conventional religious identity or plausibility structure provided a great variety of religious viewpoints and practices. The church generally approved of and even blessed, often with special indulgences, any good works and pious practices promoted by the faithful. Parishioners devoted to Mary could join a Sodality of Our Lady, be a member of the Legion of Mary, become a Slave of Mary according to the guidelines of St. Louis de Montfort, regularly attend the Tuesday night novena, pray the rosary with family daily, build grottoes, go on pilgrimages to sites of apparitions, and receive public approval (and an indulgence).

Other parishioners were attracted to devotion to the Blessed Sacrament, holy hours, and Benediction. Still others were devoted to saints or to other devotions involving scapulars and medals, ever confident of their efficacy. There were even some who managed to be preoccupied with everything available.

There was personal honor and additional security of salvation in doing something really special. If a person wanted to go the extra mile, this could be done by joining a religious community that invariably centered in some particular religious practice, devotion, or mission. For the adventurous and really contemporary lay Catholic there was the possibility of the Christian Family Movement and other lay apostolate organizations, such as the Catholic Worker movement, Extension Volunteers, Third Orders, or the newly popular Cursillo movement.

WHAT MADE THIS PLURALISM POSSIBLE?

How could this variety exist within the parish without conflict? Parishioners and parish leaders were united in how they interpreted reality, especially religious reality; they were united in their symbol system and world view. Although parishioners or their parish leaders before the 1960s did not articulate it in a formal or conscious manner, *they shared a common meaning* which was caused in large part by the formation system described above.

> ...the cohesiveness of a religious community, like every other community, is built upon common meaning. Common meaning exists when a people share more or less the same base of experiences, raise similar questions about those experiences, come to the same general understanding of the meaning of those experiences, make similar judgments about the truth and value of the common understanding of the shared experiences, and finally, follow upon those judgments with common dedication and commitment to the values and truths affirmed.[3]

What Edward K. Braxton describes here as a shared "common meaning" and Peter L. Berger describes as a "plausibility structure," Franz Jozef van Beeck, in his *Catholic Identity After Vatican II*, describes as an "arrangement of the themes and emphases of the Catholic faith and identity experience."[4] All of these expressions describe one thing: *a Catholic identity*.

From the vantage point of our experience after Vatican II we may question the religious depth and maturity of the common meaning shared by parishioners before the council. In many ways it lacked a sense of differentiation between essentials and non-essentials. On the surface it seemed centered in Latin as the language of worship, going to Mass on Sunday and not working that day, women and girls wearing hats in church, not eating meat on Friday, frequent confession (and infrequent communion), identifiable religious garb for priests and religious, external- ism, and devotionalism centered around the Blessed Sacrament, the Sacred Heart, Mary, and the saints.

At a deeper level, and probably unconscious level, it was cen- tered in *shared* images, symbols, stories, and ceremonies as the local church went about living the faith in practical ways. What we cannot deny is that a common meaning did exist, that it produced a sense of Catholic identity, and that it provided a sense of religious stability. It is described in nostalgic words: "Everything was the same. We knew what it meant to be Cath- olic. We knew what we were supposed to believe." *It is this shared common meaning that tolerated a variety precisely be- cause many different religious expressions were part of the plau- sibility structure. Regardless of what aspect of Catholicism pa- rishioners were occupied with, they knew themselves and felt themselves as Catholic. Within diversity there was unity.*

LOSS OF A SHARED MEANING
AND CATHOLIC IDENTITY

This shared Catholic identity with its innocent variety was lost in the chaotic times following Vatican II. The most impor- tant features of a religion are the words, images, symbols, sto- ries, and ceremonies or rituals. The first thing changed in wake of the council was the language of worship, from Latin to the vernacular. A renewed emphasis on public worship in the lan- guage of the people resulted in a de-emphasis on the variety of popular devotions, which were the "backbone" of pre-Vatican II spiritualities. This de-emphasis did not necessarily trans- late into practical faith in the lives of parishioners. Some clung to the old, which had given them identity and spiritual security. Others quickly discarded whatever had been, without searching for replacements.

Then the images, symbols, and ceremonies were changed by extensive reform and renewal efforts following the council, and which are still in process. The interiors of churches were re- modeled, statues removed, and old visuals stored away or destroyed. These religious "props" were as important to many people as the Baltimore Catechism definitions in providing a structure to Catholic identity. Sacraments that had been strange, mysterious, and often private ceremonies, full of effective divine power, were returned to center stage and promoted as new sources of spirituality. Extreme unction—the "Last Rites"—changed from a private introduction to death to the healing of parishioners, often publicly during the weekend liturgy. Priests and nuns who had contributed so much to the old Catholic identity began to live, act, and dress very much like the parishioners they ministered to.

Stories that had once provided a context for the old Catholic identity frequently became the object of humor and derision. Religious language, consecrated by the Baltimore Catechism, stalled to a stutter. And the Baltimore Catechism itself lost out to new catechetical theories, newly designed resource materials, and radically changed teaching methods. Lay access to the rapid advances in Scripture studies resulted in the shocking knowledge that there was no apple in Eden—and therefore what else was "only story"? Changes in the method and content of preaching challenged parishioners to come to grips with personal decisions. There would no longer be a single Catholic response. Popular theological studies—with the press publishing exciting new conclusions—continued to affect religious vocabulary and, more importantly, new priorities in religious thinking.

The result of all the changes was that parishes began *living* their faith differently. Many if not most religious traditions became irrelevant to people. A good percentage of parishioners, along with many of their spiritual leaders realized, with some lamentation, that their old story had lost much of its meaning.

Catholicism and mainstream Protestantism alike experimented with new ways and turned into some blind alleys. Theological movements competed with one another. Religious traditions and the content of popular faith, secure for centuries, were hastily shelved in favor of the new, often untested by experience and reflection. It was a time of religious, cultural, and political bandwagons and many took the ride.

A NEW PLURALISM

A new kind of pluralism began to appear in parishes: different religious convictions and practices *without a common meaning or obvious Catholic identity holding all together*. It is a pluralism that can be described with words unheard of before Vatican II: anger, aggression, stress, conflict, judgment, polarization, confrontation, etc. In light of what has been discussed so far in this chapter, these emotions are understandable. Faith had been identified for a long time with the conventional identity; therefore, changes in this identity threatened the religious security of many parishioners. The passing of their Catholic identity before a new identity could evolve was traumatic. Some aggressively held on to what had been precious to them in the pre-Vatican II conventional Catholicism, even if the official church no longer stressed it and the local parish no longer supported it. Others contributed to the new pluralistic situation with novel experiments that were "designed" rather than allowed to evolve naturally through new experiences. And still others answered a call to deeper insights into the meaning of church and its mission. These became committed to important new movements founded upon experience and gospel, even if the parish or the church at large did not concur. Each parish has its own experience of religious groups functioning separately from each other and even from the parish itself. *Ecumenism, once lacking between the Catholic church and other religions, now was lacking among Catholics themselves.*

SECTARIAN TENDENCIES

Renaming a phenomenon often contributes new insights. This is true when the dynamics of sectarianism are used to examine the parish scene today. The term "sect" is used in Protestant tradition to describe a group that breaks away from an established church. Raymond E. Brown briefly considers the notion of sectarianism in studying the pluralistic character of the early church and specifically the johannine Christians who gave birth to the fourth gospel.[5] However, taking "sectarian" in a strictly religious context, he argues that it does not apply because the religious group, the johannine Christians, did not break communion (*koinonia*) with other Christians.

Sectarianism can be examined as a sociological phenomenon, which does not necessarily preclude a total break between groups of parishioners or between these groups and the rest of the church community. Understanding the dynamics of sectarianism becomes very helpful, then, in appreciating what is happening in today's parishes:

> The term "sect" is used in different ways in common speech. Sociologically, it means a religious group that is relatively small, in tension with the larger society and closed (one might say "balled up") against it and that makes very strong claims on the loyalty and solidarity of its members. The choice to persist in defiant cognitive deviance necessarily also entails the choice of social organization.[6]

This definition of "sect" accurately describes the lived experience of parish teams trying to minister in the midst of Tridentine Catholics, charismatics, Bayside devotees, and the many other conservative and progressive groups functioning in the parish. The groups are "relatively small" in relation to the parish as a whole. They are "in tension with the larger society" of the parish, causing and experiencing stress and sometimes suspicion and conflict. Such groups become "closed against" the parish when the parish threatens their legitimacy by refusing to support their claims and agenda or by denying them any legitimacy.

One of the dynamics of sects is that adherents turn to each other, creating a social organization or a closed group high on loyalty and solidarity, legitimating for each other their interpretation of religious reality or mission. At this point in the evolution of a parish group with sectarian features there occurs a "we against them" and "we're right, you're wrong" attitude which is expressed in public statements and behavior. Often these controversies end up in press coverage and letters to the

editors. It is also at this point that a spirit of elitism and separatism solidifies group members, even though most will continue to participate in essential parish activities, including the
weekend liturgy, walking to the communion table with other
parishioners. However, it not unheard of that groups will pro-
test on the steps of the parish church.

Another sociological dynamic of sectarianism, "cognitive deviance," offers still another insight into the pluralistic tendencies in Catholic parishes during the past twenty years. "Cognitive deviance" is the choice a group makes because it fears
certain trends. It is a deliberate choice not to follow the crowd
but to go their own way and to legitimize this choice by

> ...(huddling) together with like-minded deviants—and
> huddle very closely indeed. Only in a counter-community
> of considerable strength does cognitive deviance have a
> chance to maintain itself. The countercommunity provides
> continuing therapy against the creeping doubt as to
> whether, after all, one may not be wrong and the majority
> right. To fulfill its function of providing social support for
> the deviant body of "knowledge," the counter-community
> must provide a strong sense of solidarity among its mem-
> bers.... In sum, it must be a kind of ghetto.[7]

It is hard to reflect on these words without thinking of the brief
history of some of the groups functioning in or in spite of the
Catholic parish today. If the "deviant" group is relatively
small, the tendency might be to write the members off as fanat-
ics. However, if it is a "counter-community of considerable
strength," either in size or in influence, then an altogether different parish dynamic is involved and the parish staff must
adequately meet the challenge.

The nature of a sect is to have a definite set of convictions
which cannot be compromised, a clearly identified leader who
defines reality for adherents, and a process that helps the sect
maintain its convictions and itself as a group. This is called a
"plausibility structure." Parishioners in these groups with sec-

tarian tendencies need social confirmation and affirmation for their interpretation of reality just as parishioners before Vatican II did who shared a common religious meaning or Catholic identity in the parish. When this shared religious meaning began to fade after the council, it did not take long for multiple plausibility structures to fill the vacuum, legitimizing ever new functioning religious identities and organized groups.

It is important to note that multiple plausibility structures existed in the pre-Vatican II church, legitimating every special devotion and organized religious practice. But at that time there was an overall plausibility structure holding all together. This is not the case today and therefore parishes experience a growing phenomenon with sectarian features.

Groups in the parish no longer depend entirely—if at all—on church authority figures to define religious reality as in the conventional Catholic identity before the council. In fact, it is not uncommon that groups both on the "left" and on the "right" will speak out against the pastor, the bishop, or even the pope. New "reality-definers"—a part of every plausibility structure—have appeared on the scene. These might be individuals with highly acclaimed credentials or charismatic leaders recognized only within a particular group. They can be on a continuum from a theologian like Hans Kung to a relatively unknown person claiming to see visions and receive divine messages. They can be helpful members of a parish pastoral team or a thorn in its side.

Three constituent elements of a plausibility structure[8] provide further sectarian features to groups in the Catholic parish:

1. *A supportive community of "significant others,"* who need not be relatives or close friends, though these are important. However, the significant others must be people important or personally influential to oneself. These significant others, therefore, may be a local prayer group, a chapter of the Blue Army dedicated to the message of Fatima, the 700 Club on CBN, a Marriage Encounter team, a women's support group, or even an informal group, meeting for another purpose but which supports a

particular conviction or attitude, e.g., a negative attitude toward pacifist groups.

2. *A conversational network* by which the people who are convinced of a particular religious reality keep the reality going. This term describes what happens in a particular religious group in the parish: much talking or testimony, supportive newsletters and publications, and even television—again, the example of the 700 Club. Very little is left to chance in this network of conversation. Most of the conversation in spoken word, print, or picture will be explicit in affirming, and reiterating a particular set of religious convictions.

3. *Deliberate therapeutic practices, rituals, and legitimation processes.* The purpose of these is to solidify and legitimize a particular interpretation of religious reality over and beyond its basic maintenance within a group. This basic element of a plausibility structure may include pious practices, formal rituals, a particular body of knowledge, or a special vocabulary. These provide explanation and justification for each detail of a particular religious world view or a particular functioning religious identity.

Parish ministers are very much aware of these therapeutic practices, rituals, and legitimation processes associated with parish groups: seminars, special retreats, prayer meetings, healing sessions, Marriage Encounter Weekends with their practical approach for improving marriages, pro-life demonstrations, peace and justice demonstrations, etc. Even T-shirts and bumper stickers might be used to speak to each other of common convictions within a particular sect.

Fortunately, these sectarian tendencies within Catholic parishes have not resulted in a total break between these groups and the local church. Some individuals have left the parish, but the parish team still has an opportunity—a mission—to come to grips with divergent groups because the parish is still *home* to most of them and because sectarian tendencies will more likely increase than go away.

SUMMARY

The past twenty years have seen a rapid transition from the comfortable conventional Catholic identity and unity, which all parishioners experienced, to an uncomfortable plurality of religious groups with differing convictions and practices. The pre-1960 conventional Catholic identity was produced and supported by a universal formation system that protected parishioners from outside influences. Almost every feature of this formation system was first challenged and then changed following Vatican II. The result was that parishioners, one by one or as groups, began to go in different directions religiously. Stress and conflict appeared on the parish scene. The sociological dynamics of sectarianism give insight into how divergent groups function within the parish. They tend to go their own way in strong solidarity with each other and are highly protective of convictions different from the rest of the parish. They have their own leaders, not necessarily traditional church authority figures, who define what religious reality is. They depend on an established network of speech and print and therapeutic practices.

5

ORIGINS OF THE NEW PLURALISM

In 1961, a year before the first session of Vatican II, a member of the Commission for Canon Law described the preparatory work going on by all the commissions. He summed it up: "There won't be any surprises coming from this council!" Like most church leaders and parishioners, he could not foresee that the council would become a symbolic event rather than just another highly organized and well coordinated church event. It took on a meaning and momentum neither predicted nor planned by those who prepared the agenda. It is symbolic in that it pointed to a reality other than itself. It pointed to the great shifts taking place within the cultures of the world and within theologies that had already begun to take culture into consideration.

CULTURAL SHIFT
As a result, the loss of a Catholic identity was not directly caused by Vatican II, regardless of what some nostalgic Catholics may think. It was caused, rather, by great shifts in culture, which from the time of Jesus and before have influenced religious meaning and identity. Without being expressly aware of it, parishioners before the 1960s mirrored in their practical faith the stability and predictability of the societies and cultures they lived in. However, when the foundations of their culture and society entered a period of rapid change, as it did in the 1960s, the stable, predictable, and comfortable parish began to undergo radical changes and re-interpretation.[1]

The influence of changes in culture and society on religious attitudes and practices disoriented many Catholics. Their religious formation had totally ignored, often deliberately, what was happening in the "world" around them. They could not have known that the images, symbols, stories, and ceremonies that had given them such spiritual comfort and religious identity *had been influenced by previous cultures, some of them very ancient*.

In 1972, when the effects of great cultural shifts were causing chaos throughout Western society, including post-Vatican II churches, John Powell, S.J., summarized the confusion and agony that would characterize the post-Vatican II generation and probably future generations:

> The pulse and rhythms of human life have quickened so suddenly that all who want to keep up, must run. To what we are running we cannot be sure, but we are making record time. New rhythms, no rhyme. ...How can those of a preceding generation educate those of the next generation for life if the way or style of life will be radically different? What in the past is of such permanent value that it must be transmitted? What part of the human heritage must not be lost if [people] are to remain sane and human?[2]

One cultural shift influencing religious identity today is "secularization." Attention has shifted to our "here and now" world. As a consequence, *tradition is de-emphasized*. This strikes at the soul of "that old time-religion" and Catholic identity that thrived on tradition. It is hard to keep religious traditions alive today in a parish, or for new ones to evolve, because people today do not live by tradition as intently as did their ancestors.

Parishioners today, interested primarily in the here and now world, find it *difficult to be interested in speculative truths or ultimate destinies* which once filled the pages of the Baltimore Catechism and were the outline of Sunday sermons. People now tend to be pragmatic and occupied with the task at hand. Practical gospel concerns, such as pro-life movements, peace and justice efforts, human rights efforts, concern for the poor, etc., now compete with once popular devotions. These concerns were not at the heart of the pre-Vatican II Catholic identity, though the Corporal Works of Mercy were always emphasized.

There is a new preoccupation with an *acceleration of acquiring knowledge and skills*. It is not uncommon today for parishioners to surpass the pastor in administrative, counseling, and even speaking skills. Workshops, conventions, and specialized training enable them to compete with pastors who minister out of pre-Vatican II speculative theology courses, in which a limited, detached-and-drilled-religious knowledge was prevalent. A new Catholic identity will have to take into account the explosion of religiously relevant knowledge and insights available to parishioners.

Acceleration in acquiring knowledge and skills results in *specialization*. Parish leaders, both ordained and lay, tend to be specialists in their ministry. They have a particular perspective of what is real and important. Consequently, they might be less tolerant of divergent viewpoints and practices of a "less informed" laity. Specialization has also grown within the ranks of parishioners as they acquire greater knowledge and skills related to the promotion of their particular religious viewpoint. Another effect of specialization is the evolution of support groups: pro-life, peace and justice, charismatics, traditionalists, etc.

Specialization usually results in *socialization*, the interrelationship or cooperation among the various support groups created by specialization, but so far this has been rare in the Catholic parish. A shared religious meaning or Catholic identity will continue to elude the parish unless this interrelationship and cooperation among the many functioning groups become a priority for parish leaders.

REARRANGEMENT OF THEMES OF CATHOLICISM
Although Vatican II did not directly cause the loss of a common identity among Catholics, it did inaugurate a process, far from

complete, that in effect questions the earlier Catholic identity. It called for "a significant rearrangement of the themes and emphases of the Catholic faith and identity experience."[3] This rearrangement is found in the structure and process of theological reflection. It has resulted in an adjustment of priorities in the church's mission: efforts of ecumenism, respect for religious freedom, promotion of the human rights of previously disfranchised people, promotion of a morality associated with economic and political issues, etc. Other rearrangements of themes and emphases may not seem as crucial as these, but on a practical level they disturb parishioners: de-emphasis of private devotions in favor of public worship and Scripture-oriented services, de-emphasis of externals, emphasis of personal moral responsibility and decision making, etc.

History gives warning that upheavals of this kind begin a long period of ferment—and of pluralism. This momentum is evident today and only a complete rejection of history could keep alive the hope that there will be a return to the pre-Vatican II conventional religious identity within the parish. Such hope and even considerable effort is sometimes found among parishioners savoring the past.

PROCESS APPROACH

Another reason for the loss of a shared religious identity lies in the radical shift in the way faith is interpreted and promoted. The essentialist approach, which had given credibility to the conventional Catholic identity before Vatican II, began to give way to the *process approach* after the council. "Classicist" and "historical" are other words to describe this transition in theological methodology.

Process theology, founded on the philosophy of Protestant Alfred North Whitehead (d. 1947), was made popular by Teilhard de Chardin (d. 1955). It emphasizes the dynamic movement of history and the changeability of all reality, including religious reality. While not ascribing to all the ramifications of Whitehead's theories, process thought began to influence all aspects of faith formation: theological studies, preaching, and religious education on all levels. Instead of viewing faith in a limited and static way, separated from the rest of reality, the process approach stresses the influence of history, sociology, culture, and psychology upon faith. Faith comes alive and thrives within the context of a very real world. Here a believing person experiences the great mysteries, which the essentialist approach tended to bind into correct definitions, texts, and doctrines.

The process approach is also holistic in proclaiming that there is no separation or conflict between the natural and the supernatural. Faith is human life lived to the fullest. New ways of imaging God in education and ministry quickly reflected this process approach.[4]

THE ROLE OF THEOLOGIANS

Theologians are sometimes blamed for "destroying" the pre-Vatican II Catholic identity. They are, rather, "mouthpieces of religious and cultural experiences that had been repressed far too long by the siege mentality of a Catholic Church long ill at ease both with the world she was living in *and with herself.*"[5] Years before Vatican II, prominent theologians such as Rahner and Lonergan, and the council *periti* who had been influenced by theologians such as these, had come to terms with the culture of the peoples. They and others were comfortable with the historical fact that in the past the church had existed in and had been influenced by cultures radically different from the 1960s. Therefore, Catholic identity is entirely compatible with peoples' current cultures.

An example of a theologian coming to terms with the culture of the people and with the process approach rather than the essentialist approach is Rosemary Haughton's *The Passionate God*. In her introduction to a theology of resurrection she asks:

Why am I seeing these things now? Why are the things that I am seeing going on now? And what is the reason for the intersection of the events, and my seeing them, and the kind of language available to me to express what I see? My knowledge of my own past partially answered the first question for me. My knowledge of cultural history, interpreted by means of a peculiar language I had developed for this, partially answered the second. The answer to my third question can only emerge from the assertion that true answers to fundamental human questions must have the nature of poetry.[6]

In explaining how poetry mediates the experiences of the past to the future by way of the "narrows of the present," Haughton says:

Now is a cultural moment of the most bewildering concreteness and of a totally immeasurable precision. ...And at a cultural moment when history itself was revealing, through cracks, the light of new worlds, I groped for tools to deal verbally with the extraordinary nature of what I was perceiving and found them under my untutored hands.[7]

THE ROLE OF RELIGIOUS EDUCATION

For decades the Confraternity of Christian Doctrine had been the official structure of religious instruction for young parishioners not enrolled in parochial schools. Just before the council there were widespread efforts to update CCD efforts, develop lay catechists, and promote more effective teaching techniques.

After the council there was the temptation—often yielded to—to throw out everything associated with the pre-Vatican II era. The first to go in parish after parish was the Baltimore Catechism, which had contributed most to the shared common meaning of Catholic parishioners, to their Catholic identity. Religious educators tended to go with the momentum of change, ignoring, without guilt, the fact that an effective content and method had not yet evolved nor a new direction established. A new arrangement of themes and emphases had not yet been clarified. Nor had the new goals of religious education and the ways to achieve these goals been clarified. Curricula and structures of parish programs went through repeated revisions. The result was a failure to work toward a new shared religious meaning through the efforts of the religious education ministry. Among adult parishioners there was often confusion and even anger with what seemed like—and often was—a chaotic situation.

In the late 1960s, a new minister began to appear on the parish scene: a Director of Religious Education (DRE). In parish after parish parochial schools were closed, another phenomenon of the post-Vatican II era. With hundreds more young people needing a regular religious instruction, parishes had to rethink their staffing. Monies were budgeted to hire an "expert" to direct faith formation programs, the DRE. It was common that these DREs possessed graduate degrees in religious education from an ever increasing multitude of graduate schools. Like much of religious education immediately after Vatican II, many of these graduate schools unintentionally lacked direction and stability. It was too soon to digest the great shifts occurring in culture and theology. Through no one's fault their graduates returned to parish ministry often ill-equipped to deal with the turmoil and loss of Catholic identity on the local level. Unfortunately, in some cases the DRE became a threat to groups within the parish and even to the pastor. The DRE also became a scapegoat for what seemed to be wrong in the parish.

Admittedly, the religious education movement did contribute to a breakdown in the religious security prevalent before the 1960s. It also contributed to the more progressive aspects of a new pluralism. Under administrators trained after the council it promoted the experience of freedom and creativity. It emphasized new forms of praying and worshiping. As the years passed, the ministry of religious education supported the growing concern of the church for issues of human rights, justice, and peace. Because of these efforts, along with the efforts of the blossoming liturgical and Christian service ministries, traditional features of the Catholic parish soon changed. Soon differences between parishioners who wished to preserve the past and those who were overly anxious for change were highlighted. These and other factions began to develop and to express arguments for their convictions.

IMAGINATION

Those who shared the religious meaning and conventional Catholic identity before the 1960s, living within the functioning structure of the parish, had little toleration for imagination. Although imagination was active in the devotional spiritualities of that era, it would have seemed threatening if it were used to develop new forms of ministry and new categories of religious thinking. After Vatican II the use of the imagination began to fuel and to liberate the content and methods of ministries within the parish.

> The rediscovery of the significance of the imagination for Christian faith is one of the most important events of our time. It is a struggle to return to a new and yet ancient way of experiencing and knowing, the way of myth and ritual, symbol and story, image and poetry. It is a struggle fueled by excitement, for we sense that freeing the imagination to live again could unlock new worlds and wonders for all Christians.[8]

This human power, which serves as a bridge between the ordinary dimension and the mystery dimension in all areas of life, continues to create a great variety within ministry, worship, and religious thinking. It is imagination, possibly more than anything else, that creates a difference of approach, and therefore tension, between parishioners actively preserving traditional forms of religious thinking and practices of faith and parishioners opting for change and new expressions of faith and church mission. It can excite us and lead us to explore new aspects of religious reality and new ways of being religious. This is anathema to those dedicated to preserving "what always has been."

A GENERATION LATER

The dynamics described above resulted in the loss of a commonly shared Catholic identity. While this is evident in the day to day living and ministering in the parish, it becomes publicly evident on the inter-parochial, national, and international scene. During Pope John Paul II's visit to the United States in September 1987, most factions worked together successfully in a public display of Catholic unity. At the same time, actual diversity of conviction and practice was kept before those physically present and those in the TV audience by way of protests and interviews. In a meeting between Pope John Paul II and the American bishops in Los Angeles, Archbishop John Quinn of San Francisco summed up the impact of culture and history on Catholicism in this country and on how the church understands itself, on both the local and national scene. He emphasized that faith needs to be understood and expressed "in the midst of earthly contingencies" and examined in the light of the "signs of the times." Interpreting this historic meeting, Richard McBrien said:

> The pope and the bishops were like ships passing in the night. For the most part the bishops' talks reflected a conciliar, pastoral-oriented ecclesiology. The pope's, by contrast, was preconciliar in content and juridical in tone.[9]

SUMMARY

Catholic identity and the shared common meaning that had given it foundation became fragmented in the wake of Vatican II and the world shaking changes in culture and society. Religious themes and priorities that had given the parish before Vatican II its identity were rearranged, changed, or given different emphases through the efforts of theologians and new parish ministers seeking to be in tune with new times. A stressful pluralism is now a common feature of the Catholic parish and of the church-at-large.

PART TWO

MEETING THE CHALLENGE
OF A NEW PLURALISM

6

HIERARCHY OF RELIGIOUS TRUTHS AND PRACTICES

Before Vatican II, unity with diversity was made possible by a shared religious meaning or Catholic identity. Parishes today lack this unifying bond. A deliberate effort toward developing a new Catholic identity will contribute at least a small bit to a renewed unity with a new diversity. The parish staff in its ministry is challenged today to contribute to a new Catholic identity, even though such rediscovered identity will be long in evolving, just as the old one was. It will have to be done while shifts in theology, ministry, liturgy, culture, and in the church's self-understanding continue.

In order to make this contribution toward ministry, parish ministers would benefit from 1) a familiarity with the church's hierarchy of religious truths and minister according to it, 2) a positive attitude toward pluralism and the development of effective skills or methods in promoting a shared religious meaning, which will encourage the many individuals and groups in a Catholic parish to enjoy unity in the midst of diversity.

HIERARCHY OF RELIGIOUS TRUTHS:
CLUE TO A SHARED RELIGIOUS MEANING
The National Conference of Catholic Bishops and Vatican offices quickly—perhaps too quickly—tried to deal with the loss of Catholic identity and the consequent fragmentation within

the church. They issued a flurry of documents and guidelines concerning the theory and practice of catechetics. Without saying so directly, these efforts by church authority recognize that catechesis is critical in forming a religious identity. Although the religious education director on the parish team might be more acquainted with these documents than other staff members, all would benefit from them. Religious education is a pastoral ministry and pastoral ministry is always educational in some way.

The most important of these documents are: *General Catechetical Directory*, prepared by the Sacred Congregation for the Clergy and approved by Pope Paul VI on March 18, 1971; *To Teach As Jesus Did: A Pastoral Message on Catholic Education*, prepared by the National Conference of Catholic Bishops, November 1972; *Basic Teachings for Catholic Religious Education*, prepared by the National Conference of Catholic Bishops in consultation with the Holy See, January 1973; and *Sharing the Light of Faith: National Catechetical Directory for Catholics of the United States*, prepared by the National Conference of Catholic Bishops and approved by the Sacred Congregation for the Clergy in 1979.

This latter document, NCD, is most important for the contemporary American scene. It went through three extensive consultations with lay Catholics in the United States by way of regional meetings, along with consultations with scholars and local religious educators. Widespread diversity of religious convictions in the United States resulted in tens of thousands of recommendations and extensive lobbying. The final document admittedly is a compromise with this religious pluralism; it is also a compromise with the Vatican, which approved it after changes in the text were made. Neither the NCD nor the other documents have succeeded in erasing or even mitigating the tensions of religious diversity within the national or local church. However, the wise parish worker will be familiar with this document when ministering in a pluralistic parish.

Parishioners of different, even contradictory, religious convictions often fail to take a hierarchy of religious truths into consideration. Nor do they examine their religious convictions and practices against the broader context of the church's contemporary catechesis. Therefore, it is important to examine how these documents explain and deal with such a hierarchy and what catechesis it promotes.

The NCD leaves little doubt about its purpose. It wants to present guidelines for the church's authentic teaching in light of pluralism. After several paragraphs describing problems and religious diversity within the United States Catholic church, the NCD states:

> Clearly, evangelization and catechesis are needed to solve some of these problems. The sophistication, self-awareness, and maturity with which different people approach doctrinal and moral issues vary greatly, for a variety of reasons. It is necessary to present and give witness to the Church's authentic teaching in such a way which respects the sincerity of those who are seeking to know what is true and what is right.[1]

In discussing norms for catechesis and the question of hierarchy of religious truths, the NCD adheres closely to the traditional agenda of the *General Catechetical Directory* (GCD) prepared by the Vatican's Sacred Congregation for the Clergy in 1971:

> While it is neither possible nor desirable to establish a rigid order to dictate a uniform method for the exposition of content, certain norms or criteria guide all sound catechesis. These are developed further throughout this NCD.
>
> First and foremost, catechesis is trinitarian and christocentric in scope and spirit, consciously emphasizing the mystery of God and the plan of salvation, which leads to the Father, through the Son, in the Holy Spirit. (Cf. Ephesians 1: 3-14) Catechesis is centered in the mystery of Christ. The center of the message should be Christ, true God and true man, His saving work carried out in his incarnation, life, death, and resurrection.

Since catechesis seeks to foster mature faith in individuals and communities, it is careful to present the Christian message in its entirety. It does so in such a way that the interrelationship of the elements of this message is apparent, together with the fact that they form a kind of organic whole. Thus their significance in relationship to God's mystery and saving works is best communicated.

In practice, this means recognizing a certain *hierarchy of truths* (italics mine).[2]

Then the NCD quotes this hierarchy of truths from the GCD:

These truths may be grouped under four basic heads: the mystery of God the Father, the Son, and the Holy Spirit, Creator of all things; the mystery of Christ the incarnate Word, who was born of the Virgin Mary, and who suffered, died, and rose for our salvation; the mystery of the Holy Spirit, who is present in the Church, sanctifying it and guiding it until the glorious coming of Christ, our Savior and Judge; the mystery of the Church, which is Christ's Mystical Body, in which the Virgin Mary holds the pre-eminent place."[3]

The NCD includes a clarification of the term "hierarchy":

This hierarchy of truths does not mean that some truths pertain less to faith itself than others do, but rather that some truths of faith enjoy a higher priority inasmuch as other truths are based on and are illuminated by them.[4]

This clarification provides a clue in the search for a shared Catholic identity which allows a diversity of practical expression. If "some truths of faith enjoy a higher priority," then practical expressions of faith based on these are of higher priority in the parish community. This does not mean that practical expressions of faith based on religious truths of lower priority are invalid or, worse, should be scorned by parish leaders and parishioners. They do not pertain less to faith; but neither do they enjoy as high a priority.

Parishioners might be challenged to anchor their basic Catholic identity in religious truths of higher priority. Such an identity, shared by parishioners, permits a pluralism of religious practice that reflects different emphases regarding priority truths. In sum, *a pluralism of practice expressive of lesser elements of Catholic tradition could more easily be tolerated if the basic religious identity is rooted in the higher priority truths.*

The question of "priority" refers to what the parish publicly promotes and the amount of effort and time it expends in its practical ministries of teaching, worship, community building, and service. The difficulty lies in determining this priority. Catholic tradition has always had a cornucopia of content, both official and unofficial. The other extreme is witnessed to by fundamentalist churches with their finely honed priority religious truths: five fundamentals.

A difficulty occurs when the religious priorities of the parish staff do not at all match those of parishioners in general or of individuals or groups in particular. This may be due to honest ignorance of Catholic tradition, or some form of bias. In the former case, continued catechesis may be productive. In the latter, special skills of conflict resolution, negotiation, and other public relation techniques are called for.

HIERARCHY OF TRUTHS MADE PRACTICAL

Chapter Five of the NCD, "Principal Elements of the Christian Message for Catechesis," develops the basic religious truths in ten categories, which form the core of Catholic catechesis. These categories are: one God; creation; Jesus Christ; the Holy Spirit; the church; the sacraments; the life of grace; the moral life; Mary and the saints; and death, judgment, and eternity. These ten categories remain faithful to the spirit of the hierarchy of religious truth in the GCD.

Within each of the ten categories, and in related paragraphs throughout the NCD, catechetical content reflecting both the traditional teaching of the church and some contemporary emphases is presented, sometimes in paragraphs and sometimes over pages. Thus the NCD goes beyond the narrow meaning of hierarchy of religious truth in the GCD.

This presentation of the "more outstanding elements of the message of salvation" gives evidence of compromise but favors no particular lobbying group. For this reason Chapter Five of the NCD is important as a guide for parish leaders in searching for a shared religious meaning in face of pluralism in the parish. These ten categories are reflected in the methodology provided in Part Three.

POPULAR MEANING OF HIERARCHY OF RELIGIOUS TRUTHS

The term "hierarchy of religious truths" can be—and is—used in a more popular sense. It is not difficult for most parishioners to understand that there are essentials and non-essentials within the very extensive body of Catholic teaching and traditions. It is also not difficult to understand that if we are to choose a religious truth upon which to build a spirituality that influences our daily life and leads us to meet the challenges of baptism and gospel, then this truth should be of high priority in the church's catechesis. For example, Jesus' mandate to respond to the needs of the poor commands a higher priority than private revelations, whatever their content. The location of the baptismal font is more important than the location of the votive candle stand. The parish staff can build upon this popular understanding in designing and administering programs, choosing resources, training volunteers, teaching adults, and in conducting other public and private sessions with parishioners.

The following is an example of how a consideration of a hierarchy of religious truths, both in its official and popular meaning, can help parish ministers and parishioners of different functioning religious identities to search together for a shared religious meaning. The example concerns Mary.

Mary holds a pre-eminent place in the mystery of church (GCD) and as such is part of Catholic identity. In fact, much of

Catholic tradition, official and unofficial, is related to the mystery of Mary. There are scriptural insights into a woman struggling to understand her son and herself. There are the great truths defined by councils and popes. There are popular devotions related to doctrine and Scripture. And there are popular traditions with foundations in neither doctrine nor Scripture, e.g., apparitions with a popular following.

If individual parishioners or a cluster of parishioners lobby, in private or in a public meeting, for a functioning religious identity centered in some remote aspect of the mystery of Mary, a parish staff member can take the following steps:

1. *Admit and affirm what is true.* For example, mysteries surrounding Mary, along with a wide variety of devotions to her, have been and still are a legitimate part of a Catholic identity.
2. *Listen to their story.* Patiently get a clarification of what the person or group is saying. What is the foundation of their conviction? What is the history of their religious identity? Is there any biblical or official church teaching or support related to their conviction that you can identify with and affirm? Or are they preoccupied with a religious conviction that has no substantiation in reality or that has already been discounted by church authorities (e.g., some apparitions)?
3. *Introduce the matter of a hierarchy of truths.* How much of their "religious energy" is spent on their particular preoccupation or conviction and how much on practical ramifications of mysteries with a higher priority in the church's catechesis? For example, a group wants to plan a May Crowning on Pentecost weekend. Do they see a discrepancy? Does it make sense to them? How do they justify it?

If time and opportunity allow and if they are cooperative, offer to share an official source of catechesis with them. For example, the NCD presents the principal elements of the catechesis relating to Mary in three short paragraphs in #106 and several lines in #143:

The Gospel of Luke gives us Mary's words: "My spirit finds joy in God my savior, for he has looked upon his servant in her lowliness; all ages to come shall call me blessed." (Lk 1:47f) The "ever-virgin mother of Jesus Christ our Lord and God" occupies a place in the Church second only to that of Christ. Mary is close to us as our spiritual mother.

Singularly blessed, Mary speaks significantly to our lives and needs in the sinlessness of her total love. Following venerable Christian tradition continued in the Second Vatican Council, the Church recognizes her as loving mother, its "model and excellent exemplar" in faith and charity.

The special gifts bestowed on her by God include her vocation as mother of God, her immaculate conception (her preservation from original sin), and her entry into Christ's resurrection in being assumed body and soul to heaven. The special love and veneration due her as mother of Christ, mother of the Church, and our spiritual mother should be taught by word and example.

...the rosary of the Blessed Virgin Mary (is associated with) the months of May and October. In fact, with the multiplicity of ethnic and cultural backgrounds, devotions to the Lord, the virgin and the saints provide a rich tapestry on which is woven the many threads of our ancestry in the faith.

4. *Invite the person(s) to examine the matter further.* The first situation is often a heated one accompanied by stress. A second session may allow for some compromise and the beginning of mutual understanding and respect, even though basic convictions continue.

THE NCD AS A PRACTICAL DOCUMENT

Not every parish worker will find everything in the NCD to her or his liking. In some aspects it is a very progressive document; in other aspects it represents a more conservative approach. It does encourage the use of the behavioral sciences in ministry and adopts contemporary findings with respect to faith and human development. It is conservative in its treatment of traditional morality, especially sexual morality, but is progressive in supporting the morality of peace and social justice. As is true of all official guidelines and documents, the NCD needs to be interpreted. In some cases the momentum of the diocese or parish is already an interpretation.

SUMMARY

In order to minister effectively in the midst of pluralism parish ministers need to be familiar with and make practical the hierarchy of truth within the church's catechesis and the content and directions of this catechesis. For our generation this catechesis is summarized in Chapter Five and related paragraphs of the NCD.

7

ATTITUDE AND SKILLS

Parish ministers do not have an easy task in dealing with pluralism. Besides being familiar with and functioning from within the church's hierarchy of religious truth and contemporary catechesis, they need to have a *positive attitude toward pluralism and effective skills in promoting a unity within diversity*. The challenge is to promote and coordinate expressions of orthodox belief and practice in the parish without undue stress and conflict.

TOLERANCE
The present situation of pluralism in the Catholic parish, accompanied by stress and conflict, calls for a healthy attitude of *tolerance*. Otherwise, further fragmentation will increase. Only those parish leaders and parishioners of open mind and willing heart can build—or rebuild—the local church. In an article dealing with the rebuilding of pluralistic parishes, John R. Zaums discusses two rules for tolerance, which he borrows from Reinhold Niebuhr: 1) to be willing to seriously consider divergent views without making an effort to condemn or suppress them, and 2) to develop the ability to remain true to and act from one's best convictions and understanding of truth while, at the same time, seriously considering opposing views.

But in order for us to learn these lessons of tolerance, we must continually reflect and act upon the belief that we are a *pilgrim people*. The idea of a pilgrim Church connotes, in a general way, the Church's imperfect and incomplete state. To say that the Church is on a pilgrimage means that it has not yet reached the fullness of glory, which is its final goal. The law of its earthly existence is a law of development, a law of growth and continual reform.[1]

Only through the virtue of tolerance will parish ministers and the parish as a united whole understand diversity as a strengthening factor rather than a source of antagonism. Tolerance becomes the bridge that brings together the separated factions in the parish. It opens the door to representatives of different factions serving together on councils and committees. It welcomes parishioners of opposing views to work together in planning parish liturgies and activities. Sometimes the heat of conflict cools when opposing viewpoints are permitted an airing or hearing. Not everyone will get their way, but everyone can have their say.[2]

PATIENCE AND COMPROMISE

Other Christian virtues are challenged during a time of pluralism. One of these is *patience*. As Karl Rahner has observed in discussing the matter of pluralism in the church, sometimes "all the Christian can do is come to terms with the situation, bear it patiently, and maintain in the church a unity which is effective in practice in spite of the difficulties involved."[3]

Besides working patiently for unity, Rahner also suggests the need to *compromise* but without a "sham peace" and sometimes allowing for a "fair fight":

> ...compromises simply cannot be avoided: they merely reflect the facts and try to do justice as far as possible to all these non-simultaneous groups. Since all the groups in principle certainly have a right to exist, the fact must be accepted in teaching and in practice that in the one Church with her one Spirit there can and must be a variety of charisms whose ultimate harmony perhaps simply cannot be fully experienced by us in the still continuing

course of history; and [the Spirit] is not identical either with any sort of individual group or with the Church's of-fice-holders. The legitimacy of such compromises to main-tain the Church's unity in the diversity of historically non-simultaneous groups cannot, of course, mean a sham peace and does not remove the necessity of a fair fight among the groups.[4]

Rahner also emphasizes the need for *self-criticism*. Those who minister in parishes know the stubbornness that exists among particular religious groups as each tries to legitimize its exis-tence and lobby for its convictions. However, the harshness and even bitterness that accompanies the struggle can be kept with-in tolerable limits "if each group is self-critical and tries to un-derstand the other group, if people are not too quick to deny the good will or genuine Christianity of both sides."[5]

Self-criticism does not mean that one's convictions are inval-id. Methods used to express those convictions, however, are al-ways open to question and critique. So, too, is one's personal at-titude toward the "opposition party." A particular group in the parish, out of love for tradition or opposition to diocesan litur-gical guidelines, may oppose the pastor's and parish council's intentions to remodel their parish church. This personal convic-tion—for them—is legitimate. The authority of the pastor and parish council is also legitimate. From this point on, as each side separately and together works toward resolution, self-criticism is of the highest importance. "Is it a legitimate Christian thing for us to do to gain control of the parish council for the expressed purpose of preventing the remodeling? To ini-tiate a law suit against the bishop? To call in the secular press?" On the other hand, "Is it a legitimate Christian thing for us to do to hold secret meetings of the building committee to complete plans before the opposition can muster support?"

FACILITATING HEALING
Jacques Weber, S.J., in considering the frustrations of dealing with Catholic fundamentalists, one example of a functioning

religious identity in today's parish, offers positive suggestions to facilitate healing and growth.[6] The same suggestions are valid in dealing with other functioning religious groups. (Blanks occur where Weber's text has "Catholic Fundamentalists.")

1. Mockery toward____must be excluded from the thinking and feeling of pastoral leaders. Rather, compassion and a search for understanding are essential.
2. Pastoral leaders must do their best not to turn away from____. The risk of dialogue should be taken. Yet pastoral leaders have a right to their own private space and respect. On these they can and should insist without actively turning away from____ who are, in many cases, friends and colleagues.
3. Decide who has the problem. Making such a conscious decision puts the relationship in perspective and helps pastoral leaders to avoid feelings of being threatened.
4. Remember that____can be aggressive and sometimes disruptive in public meetings. Pastoral leaders, therefore, must remain in charge even while they are trying to create a democratic climate for dialogue and reconciliation. A call to prayer can frequently quell a stressful situation. Pastoral leaders have a right and even an obligation to call to prayer when the occasion demands it.
5. Focus the problem. The fear, anger, and other deep feelings they have are often unfocused. Though often rooted in a pattern of past experiences, these hostile feelings are frequently free floating. If the real issue can be focused there is a chance for productive dialogue. Some focusing questions are: Is one experiencing fear of change? Or a desire to control? Or a need to be taken seriously and understood?

THEOLOGICAL REFLECTION
Theological reflection is an important skill for parish ministers.[7] It is a corporate process of listening, communicating, and decision making. The word "corporate" is not an incidental adjective. It emphasizes the *group* process instead of the solitary—even though learned and specially experienced—voice.

The question always is: "What is the group saying?"

Theological reflection makes use of three sources of information that are religiously relevant: tradition, experience, and culture. This process is quite comprehensive and, therefore, an excellent tool in coming to grips with the tensions and conflicts within the parish. It avoids the less than desirable "quick fix" approach. The goal of theological reflection is not solely to promote a clarification of thinking within a group, though it does this; the goal is to come to a pastoral decision or a ministerial response regarding a particular situation.

In this corporate process the participants first of all identify all the information they can think of from tradition (Scripture, church history, church teaching) concerning a particular pastoral concern or stress issue. This is "tossed into the hopper" (or on the chalkboard) without deep reflection at this point. To this is added all the information available to the participants from their experience and from culture and society that speaks to the issue being discussed. For example, in reflecting upon the role of the laity in church ministry and worship, it would be naive to consider only past church discipline and traditions. The experience of the laity themselves and their giftedness played out in their cultural setting need to be considered as part of what the mystery of church is called to be today.

Once the relevant information has been gathered, the process continues:[8]

1. Private reflection on the issue(s) in light of the accumulated information.
2. Sharing in a group the fruits of this private reflection (not a group discussion)...corporate listening (where does the group hear agreement?)...lobbying (individual statements to persuade others), again not a discussion or debate.
3. Listing of points of agreement and disagreement.
4. Is there sufficient agreement to act? If yes, then process is finished. If no, then the areas of agreement are set aside and the entire process is repeated.

The process ends when there is sufficient agreement to act or when the group finds it impossible to move toward any agreement.

Theological reflection does not automatically resolve situations. Several hurdles will be evident almost immediately. The greatest of these are the different ways participants approach tradition. Some might view Scripture in a fundamentalist fashion. Parish ministers will probably approach it from an historical or critical angle. Some will approach church teaching as if everything is *de fide*. Others might tolerate church teaching only in a highly critical fashion. *Theological reflection succeeds only if there is respect for a plurality of convictions.*

RITUAL SPEAKING

An important act of tolerance—and skill—is to *listen* to a person who speaks from a different religious conviction. Understanding "ritual speaking"[9] is helpful if a parish team member wishes to cope with pluralism. Parishioners use a particular language to describe their religious experiences and convictions and to lobby for them.

Rituals of action and language are normative in the history of religions. They preserve and transmit the heart of a religious experience enjoyed by an individual, a religious group, or a religious movement. A person who enjoys a religious experience or is preoccupied with a particular religious conviction naturally wants to talk about the meaning of that experience or conviction with others.

Ritual speaking uses a particular vocabulary with emphasis on certain patterns of religious words and catch phrases by which persons communicate their convictions to others. Parishioners' religious language is, therefore, an indication of their religious conviction and preoccupation. It describes them religiously.

For example, charismatics tend to use joyous and emotional language to describe a new and profound experience of the Spirit and personal changes because of that experience. Sometimes, however, the language used may have a subtle nuance. Charismatics with a fundamentalist bent may use the term "Christian" and limit the term to a person who has experienced a baptism in the Spirit or a "born again" experience. In their conversation they might also describe, and limit, an activity as "Christian" only if it is done by a re-born person or group. A parish minister is challenged to listen carefully and to ask questions to clarify the intent of the language.

Ultra-conservative parishioners or traditionalists will often use words reminiscent of a pre-Vatican II era and the Baltimore Catechism, which characterized that era. The parish minister may have little difficulty in recognizing this and putting it into perspective, but conservative factions may also use subtle "authority" or "parent" expressions (should, have to, supposed to, not allowed to, etc.). In this case, without realizing the cause, the minister may react negatively to this "harsh parenting" as an angry or rebellious child of long ago.

Quite often, therefore, parishioners may use an explicit language of religious preoccupation, which is not difficult to recognize, and a subtle language that calls for more effort on the part of the listener to understand. For example, Blue Army devotees will speak about the visions at Fatima and Mary's message to pray the rosary for the conversion of Russia. Their subtle language might imply that the efforts of peace groups are of no use. On the other hand, peace groups may be very outspoken about the gospel call to active peacemaking and subtly imply that prayer for peace is a lower priority.

Ritual speaking has been part of every religious identity since the "first day of the week" (an example of ritual speaking) when friends and followers experienced Jesus with new life and still with them. The ritual speaking of early Christianity still echoes for us in the pages of Scripture. It continued to evolve as the church journeyed through history. Sometimes controversy about a core belief of Christians affected religious speech. How to speak about the mystery of Jesus? the Trinity? the inner life of God? The early councils of Nicea (325), Ephesus (431), and Chalcedon (451) provided the christological and trinitarian religious language still traditional today. The Medieval essentialist interpretation of Thomism and the counter-Reformation period ushered in by Trent (1545-1563) produced the ritual speech still common in the church in the mid-twentieth century.

Ritual speaking is not limited to the inspired Scriptures, official church doctrine, theologies, or catechisms. It is also the vehicle that describes and transmits popular spiritualities and functioning religious identities from people to people and from generation to generation: the veneration of saints, the use and veneration of blessed objects, devotions to Mary, adherence to private revelations from visionaries, popular understanding of the sacraments, etc. Such ritual language takes place in various ways: in the pulpit, at retreats, in books and brochures, at meetings, in prayer groups, and in private conversations.

Vatican II greatly influenced the way Catholics speak about the mysteries of faith. The council spoke emphatically and in new ways about the mystery of the church and her mission in the world. People, for example, now freely speak of a "pilgrim church," "collegiality," and "ministry."

Popular movements of our times—biblical, liturgical, charismatic, peace and justice, pro-life, parish renewal, and women's equality—challenge the conventional ways of speaking about religious matters. These movements have already produced a ritual language that is becoming more and more common among parishioners: liturgy instead of Mass, lectors, greeters instead of ushers, proclamation of the word, literary forms, healing, prophecy, speaking in tongues, liberation, pro-life, small groups, base communities, inclusive language, etc. There is hardly a parish that has not been influenced, some perhaps by rejecting it, by the ritual speaking within the new pluralism.

INADEQUACY OF RITUAL SPEAKING

Neither official nor popular religious language can adequately capture the full reality of religious matters. The dimension of mystery exceeds the limits of any attempt to capture it in words. Like all rituals, ritual speaking can only point to and make us aware of the mysteries so that we can experience them in the depths of our selves. Yet it is not unusual for individuals and groups to presume that because they speak the words, they possess the reality, and that because they speak the words to another, the other should accept the reality.

Even in cases where many speak the same religious language, there is no guarantee that the reality spoken about is identical:

> As I listen to another's religious words, I am never sure they express the same inner experience those words evoke in my life. Since my inner experience is the criterion for understanding the truth of my relationship with God, the words of another person cannot really summon me to reform this relationship.[10]

In addition to being inadequate, ritual speaking is not a pure communication form. When we talk about our faith and share it with others, for example in the context of catechetical ministry, we cannot stay completely within one particular tradition. The words used will ordinarily be from a healthy mixture of functioning religious identities: conventional, contemporary, scriptural, liturgical, charismatic, etc. This is where the church is at present and it is natural that the way we speak about religious truths reflect the current situation.

People who lock themselves into only one way of speaking about religious matters effectively block communication. One of the curses of current pluralism within the Catholic parishes, is that *parishioners often cannot talk with one another because they cannot understand or will not listen to another way of talking about religious matters*. This difficulty, even frustration, parallels situations in which members of mainline churches try to communicate with fundamentalists. They are not speaking the same language. Communication is blocked.

RITUAL SPEAKING AND THE PARISH MINISTER
Some parish ministry might seem to involve ritual speaking more than others. For example, almost the entire ministry of

catechetics concerns ritual speaking in some way: actual cate-
chising opportunities, catechist training, public and private
meetings with parents, adult catechumenate and other adult
formation sessions, etc. But in reality all parish ministry in-
volves ritual speaking, since individuals and groups speak differently about religious convictions. The entire parish team has
opportunities, therefore, to make a contribution to a positive
pluralism by listening carefully and speaking in such a way
that there is movement toward a shared meaning rather than
away from it.

Parish ministers' ritual speaking should reflect, first of all,
their own religious experiences and religious convictions. No
one benefits from faking or covering up one's own spiritual reality. During the present time of transition, however, it is important that parish ministers clarify as well as possible their own
functioning religious identity and develop a clarity of speech
about it. There should not be an unbridgeable communication
gap between parish ministers and parishioners. Instead of over-
whelming (and confusing) an individual or group with new
words, there should be patience in explaining terms, sometimes
using an older language until an idea is grasped and a newer
language is appreciated. Avery Dulles puts this challenge very
succinctly: "Could not many impasses be transcended...if adherents of different religious traditions made an effort to appre-
ciate one another's symbol systems?"[11]

Faith is internal and usually lasting, but the words by
which it is expressed are always external and transitional.
This is humbling both for those who stubbornly hold on to a pre-
Vatican II language and for those who think they have invent-
ed the best and final way of speaking about religious reality.
Parish workers need to relax, therefore, when hearing a different ritual language. The world will not end because we hear old
words and others hear new words.

SUMMARY
The parish minister must be willing to consider divergent views
without condemning or suppressing them, and at the same time

remain true to and act upon one's best convictions and experiences of truth. The parish minister should be acquainted with some basic negotiating, group sharing, and public relations tools to facilitate healing and communication. The parish minister should be patient, able to compromise, but also have the stomach for a "fair fight." Finally, the parish minister needs to listen carefully to those speaking out of a different religious experience and be able to interpret correctly the language used.

PART THREE

A CASE STUDY
METHODOLOGY

8

INTRODUCTION TO CASE STUDIES

The issues discussed in Parts One and Two can be summed up in five statements:

1. There always has been and always will be a tension between theory and practice as the church tries to understand itself and live up to its calling through individual Catholics, organized groups, and parishes.
2. Throughout the history of the Catholic church this tension has resulted in a diversity of functioning religious identities as the norm rather than the exception.
3. Unity within diversity in parishes before Vatican II was possible because parishioners shared a common religious meaning or Catholic identity.
4. The situation of stress, conflict, and division in parishes after Vatican II is rooted in the loss of this shared meaning or Catholic identity and the evolution of groups with sectarian features.
5. Parish ministers are in a position to contribute to a unity within diversity by representing and promoting a positive attitude toward diversity of religious convictions and practices, by using effective skills in ministering in the midst of this diversity, and by actively contributing to a shared religious meaning among Catholic parishioners.

There is no one particularly effective method that will promote a positive pluralism in the parish. Part Two concentrated on some attitudes and skills that can serve as basic tools for the parish team. Part Three now concentrates on a particular methodology: a coordinated response to fictitious cases. This methodology can be used to train team members to minister more effectively in the midst of divergent viewpoints and practices. It can also be an effective methodology for training parish councils and committee members, and for other adult groups.

OBJECTIVES
The case study methodology presented here has four objectives:

1. To challenge parish ministers to clarify their own functioning religious identity, along with the personal history behind this identity.
2. To enable parish ministers to deal more effectively with the stress and conflict caused by the diversity of religious thinking and practice in the parish. This is done by encouraging an honest variety of emotional and ministerial responses within a group to fictitious cases that describe stress situations.
3. To encourage parish ministers to foster unity within diversity by working toward a shared religious meaning or Catholic identity with parishioners of different religious convictions. This is done by inviting participants to consider the basic catechetical content from the *National Catechetical Directory* (NCD) and related sources in responding to the fictitious cases. This emphasis on the NCD *does not exclude* reflection and discussion centered in Scripture, tradition, and experience.
4. To familiarize parish ministers with the case study technique as a tool that might be used on the local level to train volunteer workers with some form of public ministry, such as catechists and Christian service volunteers, and to challenge parishioners to take a more comprehensive approach toward contemporary pluralism.

STRUCTURE OF THE METHODOLOGY
Case studies can easily be adapted to any parish ministry: administration, religious education, liturgy, Christian service,

etc. While it would benefit the individual reader to be challenged by this methodology, the author's intent is that it be
used in a group setting where the actual feeling of dealing with
different viewpoints is possible.

INTRODUCTORY SEMINAR

If the cases are used as a training program or to challenge parishioners, it is advised that they be preceded by several hours
of introduction to serve as a context. Such an introductory seminar would summarize Parts One and Two with special emphasis
on the summary statements at the beginning of this Part Three.
After this introduction the participants should be guided in examining their own functioning religious identity so that they
might begin the case studies fully aware of their own convictions. The following are some key questions to help participants
to do this:

1. How would you describe yourself as a religious person to
someone else?
2. Which religious truths are most important to you, i.e. what
religious reality do you tend to rally around? How does this affect your practical faith?
3. Which individuals or groups have been most influential in
the defining of your religious reality? How have they done
this?
4. Paraphrase a couple of your favorite Scripture verses or pas-
sages and explain why they are important to you.
5. Describe your favorite way of praying and how it fits into
your life.
6. Describe the most pressing moral issues in the world today.

It is understandable if participants find it difficult to come
to grips with their own functioning religious identity. The narrow attitudes and proselytizing or lobbying efforts of some fundamentalists, charismatics, and other groups in the parish
have "turned off" some parish ministers. This frustration often
leads to an attitude of "I don't want to be like them!" which, in

turn, sometimes translates into a lack of clarity about one's own personal convictions. This haziness about religious convictions—understandable in a period of transition—might also be the result of "overload" from workshops, conventions, reading of contemporary literature, and other professional and personal stress.

Many groups in the parish have a plausibility structure that clearly defines what is believed, what ritual language is used, and how one is to live. The point is not to imitate the definite but sometimes narrow convictions of these groups, but rather to clarify one's religious convictions and the foundations of one's spirituality to serve as the context for ministry and, when called for, the context for communicating with those of differing convictions.

ADVANTAGES OF CASE STUDIES
The case study methodology promises to be an effective tool in dealing with pluralism because participants will ordinarily represent at least slightly differing functioning religious identities. Fictitious case studies, because they are objective, allow all to examine the issues without having to defend oneself. The case study methodology, therefore, has a chance to be effective without causing even greater stress and conflict. A further advantage of using case studies is that it creates a condition outside of self and thus frees participants to look at issues more clearly and with a minimum of bias. Each case study can also become an open door for discussions of related issues. Small and large group sessions following private reflection become a bridge to other people's ideas and experiences.

CONTENT
Fifteen situations are presented here in Part Three. All of them are fictitious so that no particular crisis or parish can be identified by the participants. It should be understood that these cases are left open-ended to allow a variety of solutions, responses, and clarifications. They are, therefore, not complete stories.

The content of the fifteen cases reflects *some* of the situations causing stress and conflict in Catholic parishes. The first five cases deal with cluster pluralism, which was defined in Chapter 1 as the kind where religious preoccupation is accompanied by some aspects of organization: identification with each other in the cluster, meetings, mutual support activities, some link to a broader group, regional or national conventions, and a tendency to lobby viewpoints privately with others or more publicly at parish meetings. There are many examples of cluster pluralism, both progressive and conservative. The situations here are limited to: 1) charismatics with extreme tendencies, 2) Catholic traditionalists such as Catholics United for the Faith, 3) pro-life groups with a limited agenda, 4) highly agitated groups organized against some particular parish administrative decision, and 5) extreme Marian devotees such as Bayside devotees.

Besides these five, one case study is devoted to each of the ten categories of religious truths developed in the NCD, Chapter Five: "Principal Elements of the Christian Message for Catechesis." This disproportionate number of cases reflects the thesis that it is important for parish leaders and parishioners to keep in mind the catechesis of the church and its hierarchy of religious truth. A methodology that includes the principal elements of the church's catechesis might lead to a shared religious meaning contributing to a new Catholic identity—a new unity within diversity.

STRUCTURE OF THE CASE STUDIES
This methodology can be adapted to any time frame. Ideally, each case study will cover at least one hour:

1. Twenty minutes for reading and private reflection on the following issues related to the case:
   a. emotional reaction to the case situation
   b. different forms of ritual language and ways of living the religious conviction indicated in the case
   c. the effect of the case situation on parish life
   d. how the participants would react in a similar situation
   e. possibilities of movement toward a common religious meaning through a consideration of the NCD and other sources

    f. experiences of similar situations in the participants' own
ministries
2. Twenty minutes for small group sharing
3. Twenty minutes for large group sharing

An opportunity to respond follows each case. Participants
record briefly how they relate to some of the above issues.
These reflections are then used in small group and large group
sharing.

This structure of the case studies can be varied at will. Most
of the situations are in dialogue form; therefore, role playing
instead of private reading can be used as an option. Another option is to skip the small group sharing in favor of the large
group for a spontaneous reaction to the case.

ROLE OF THE PERSON CONDUCTING THE CASE STUDIES

While presenting the opening seminar and coordinating the
structure of the case studies, the presenter/coordinator should
encourage the participants to contribute to a positive pluralism
within the parish by meeting the following challenges:

1. To stay in touch with the reality of the church as it lives its
calling in contemporary society. No one in the parish will benefit from compromises that deny the reality around us. For example, increased emphasis on the role of women is a growing issue
both in society and in church ministries. To claim that this issue does not, or should not, exist will not be of benefit to any
movement toward unity within diversity.
2. To represent the church's basic calling and identity. This
would include an adequate insight into the history of the
church and its teaching. For parish ministers of this generation,
the church's "basic calling and identity" is also represented
by—besides Scripture—the documents of Vatican II, recent en-
cyclicals, guidelines and pastoral letters from the Vatican, National Council of Catholic Bishops, local bishops, and diocesan
offices. One of the most helpful of these documents for its prac-
ticality and comprehensiveness is the *National Catechetical*

Directory. Admittedly, this directory has some weaknesses, including compromises caused by pluralism. Still, it can be a guide toward a shared religious meaning and Catholic identity. Like all church documents, the NCD needs to be interpreted.[1] The local church, diocesan and parish, may already be experiencing a momentum that identifies "the basic experience out of which the church lives." This is an interpretation of the NCD and gives direction to what the parish minister represents in contributing to a shared religious meaning. In brief, responses to the case studies, as actual ministry itself, should avoid both extremes: that church documents are inspired like Scripture, or that they do not exist.

3. To stay in touch with one's own insights that result from a continued search for meaning during this period of transition in the church. Participants in the case studies should be invited to share these insights and to act upon them in their actual ministry.

RESPONSE QUESTIONS

Each situation presented here in Part Three is followed by a series of questions that encourages participants to deal with a situation adequately. This is often difficult to do in the day-to-day practical reality of ministry, another advantage of the case study methodology. The opportunity to reflect upon one's feelings is very important because it avoids turning the effort into an ineffective head trip. Private reflection, followed by small and large group discussion, allows the participants to focus on any one of the many issues relating to the case; for example, in responding to an extreme form of the charismatic movement in Situation One, participants might find themselves discussing the meaning of prayer and different methods of praying.

MAKING UP NEW CASES

It is not intended that this methodology be limited to the cases provided here in Part Three. One of the easiest ways to provide new—and current content—is to lift stories and articles directly from newspapers with names and locations deleted (cf. Situation Four). When doing so, several things should be kept in mind. First, the intended use needs to be clarified. Is the case to be used to initiate a process of actual conflict resolution? Or, is it to be used to open up new issues? Or, is the case to be used for some precise purpose such as exploring the role of women in the church? The intended use will determine which resources the parish minister will need to be acquainted with. Unless the intended use is clarified and the parish minister well prepared, the methodology could result in stirring up confusion and result in even more stress. A case study exercise need not result in clear resolution of a situation, but it should result in a positive direction, such as an improved attitude.

SPECIAL RESOURCES
Sometimes special resources should be available in using the case study methodology. The primary source for the cases in Situations Six through Fifteen might be the NCD if the primary objective is to move toward a shared religious meaning. Another excellent resource is Richard P. McBrien's *Catholicism* (Study Edition, Minneapolis: Winston Press, 1981). The special value of McBrien's book is that it provides a multiple context for each aspect of Catholicism: Scripture, history of dogma, philosophy, history, psychology, etc.

At times a particularly qualified resource person or the availability of printed/audio/video special resources are important. "Winging it" may have unfortunate results entirely contrary to the purpose of the methodology. For example, Situation Two on the surface concerns the anxiety of conservative Catholics. However, a deeper issue is that of women's role within the church. This is an example of such an important issue that adequately prepared resource persons and special reference materials should be available. No one parish minister can be an expert on every issue challenging the church today.[2]

IMPLICATIONS OF THE CASE STUDY METHODOLOGY
Careful observation of the responses to the fictitious cases will reveal emotional layers that color actual conflicts between pa-

rishioners of different religious convictions or between parish staff members and deviant religious groups. It is helpful to the participants' actual ministry to be aware of the implications of the emotional overtones of their discussions of the cases (and recorded on their responses to the situations). A brief introduction to "transactional analysis" made popular by Eric Berne, M.D.[3] will make this implication clearer.

Briefly, transactional analysis deals with the three ego states of each person, two of which are a *re-playing* in present situations or transactions, of the emotions attached to and recorded in early childhood situations:

1. *Child*: hungry for discovery and sensation, but also a product of all the disapproval, punishment, fears, and other negative feelings brought on by confrontations with parents and other adults.
2. *Parent*: huge collection of rules, moral dictums, and how-to-do-it instructions provided for each child.
3. *Adult*: the juggler of intense feelings and needs of the "child" and the rules and mandates of the "parent," similar to a data processing center that sorts through, and keeps one aware of, what's going on inside and outside while interacting with others. This ego state is gradually *learned*.

These ego states "play out" as people interact. Sometimes there is evidence of an excited and playful or frightened and rebellious *child*, sometimes of a fingerpointing *parent*, and sometimes, hopefully, a clear-headed and mature *adult*. How these ego states play out in stress situations caused by pluralism in the parish can lead to helpful insights. Briefly, the temptation is to act out of the "child" state (e.g., hurt or rebellious) or the "parent" state (e.g., telling someone who they should be and what they should believe and how they should live religiously). The challenge is to stay in the "adult" state (with a healthy dose of the happy "child") in dealing with a person or group of a differing functioning religious identity and to invite the other to do the same. Otherwise, there will be little progress in communication and little respect for one another's convictions.

It is not difficult to answer rather comfortably out of the "adult ego state" when dealing with a somewhat theoretical question such as: "If you were the administrator in this situation, what would you do?" However, if the question is changed to: "How would you *feel* if you were in a similar situation?" the answers (as in actual situations in the parish) will reflect many "angry child" and some "parent" tapes playing out. The following are some examples:

Child: I would feel threatened...angry...deflated...overwhelmed...sad...inadequate...frustrated...unprepared...defensive...terribly surprised...upset...worried...hurt...helpless...futile...not qualified for my job...very sorry...mad...heart would be pounding...perplexed...fearful.

Parent: I would use my authority...church should be a peacemaker...I feel that____is wrong...guilt that I hadn't ministered to his needs better...I don't think____is open to any discussion...how sly of them!...isn't this stupid! ...offended...not very tolerant...shocked.

SUMMARY

If pluralism always has been and still is the norm in the history of the church, then the parish minister is invited to react positively in its presence in the contemporary parish. The challenge then becomes not how to *eradicate* pluralism but how to put it *into context*, to live with it, and to minister in the midst of it. The case study methodology is a step in that positive direction.

9

A MONTH OF CRISES

St. Paul Parish
Fr. Gene, the Pastor
Molly, Director of Religious Education
Sr. Peg, the Liturgist
Tom, the Christian Service Coordinator

These fifteen situations portray ministry as a challenge for the parish staff. They are a small sample of the stress and conflict caused by divergent viewpoints and practices in Catholic parishes today. Each situation is deliberately open-ended, and is followed by a brief process to examine and to improve a staff person's emotional, theological, and ministerial response in a pluralistic parish.

Situation One
A SPIRIT RELEASED
This has not been Molly's week! Mrs. Green showed up at a weekend confirmation retreat for the teens of the parish. In front of all the retreatants she called down the Holy Spirit on the parish center "so that our teens might find the Lord." During the retreat she returned and, with some companions kneeling in the hallway with arms outstretched, conducted a prayer vigil.

Mrs. Green, a professional person who owns her own business, is one of many charismatics in the parish. Molly has good relations with most of them and considers their faith and enthusiasm an asset to parish life. Several are catechists. But Mrs. Green is another story! She manages to become part of every parish event and attends most meetings, always lobbying for her convictions and freely talking about her religious experiences. Before her "baptism in the Spirit," she had very little to do with the parish and in fact has little background in Catholic traditions.

Mrs. Green is an active member of a local ecumenical prayer group that sometimes meets in the parish center. At least once a week she attends an Assembly of God church, in her own words, "to get a spiritual shot in arm" not provided by the parish. She speaks in tongues frequently and has encouraged her children to do the same in their religious education sessions. On occasion at parish meetings she will deliver what she calls "God's prophecies" for the parish.

This morning she walked into the education office and questioned the effectiveness of Molly's ministry among the teens of the parish. She told Molly that two of the teens had already joined the Assembly of God church and her own daughter was thinking of doing the same. She asked to join the parish confirmation team so that she could share with the teens her own experience of the Spirit. She also urged Molly to invite the teen evangelization group from the Assembly of God to help the teens of the parish "to find out that they can have fun with the Lord." She gave Molly some literature about the evangelization team and asked that Molly get back to her so that she can make the arrangements. She also wanted to know when the confirmation team meets.

Response

1. Pretending you are Molly, describe your feelings toward Mrs. Green as the situation unfolds.
2. Still pretending that you are Molly, when Mrs. Green has made her requests and finally leaves your office, do you already know what your decision will be? Why? Why not?
3. What do you consider to be the core issue in this situation:

what Mrs. Green believes or how she practices her convictions?
How important is this distinction?
4. What religious meaning shared by Molly and Mrs. Green
might be developed as common ground for future communication?
5. How does I Corinthians 14:1-40 speak to this situation?
6. What have you experienced in your ministry that is compar-
able to this situation? How did you handle it?

Situation Two
SPYING ON THE FREEDOM WE ENJOY
For several years some parishioners have been suggesting to the
parish council that there be a May Crowning on Mother's Day,
"like in the old days." This year Fr. Gene suggested that Sr. Peg
work it out with the liturgy commission and the young people in
the religious education programs.

With the liturgy commission Sr. Peg developed a creative
alternative to the traditional crowning of a statue with flowers
by a little girl. They developed a liturgy celebrating the theme
of *woman*, convinced that Mary lived perfectly what it means
to be female in human life and in God's service.

As the liturgy unfolded this weekend, parishioners were met
with women greeters at the door, women ushers, girls serving
Mass, a woman lector, and a guest woman preacher who is pastor at a Methodist church. In his introduction Fr. Gene pointed
out the fruitful contribution by women to the life of St. Paul
parish. The woman preacher developed the theology of women
in ministry. She also joked that maybe Fr. Gene wasn't necessary any more.

Then came the "crowning." Six women representing each age
level, from a girl in the second grade to a senior citizen, stood
before the microphone and testified to what Mary must have
felt at that age level. There was a spontaneous applause before
the liturgy continued. Sr. Peg was especially pleased to see
some very conservative parishioners seated close to the front of
the church. They even took pictures.

Then the bomb was dropped. When Sr. Peg told Fr. Gene how

pleased she was that conservatives were there and even took pictures, he laughed and said: "Those were C.U.F. (Catholics United for the Faith) members and by now the pictures and a report including our names are on the way to Rome!"

A half-hour ago a parish representative of this C.U.F. group made an appointment to meet with Sr. Peg.

Response
1. Pretend that you are a member of C.U.F. How do you feel about Sr. Peg and the liturgy commission? Why do you feel this way?
2. Still pretending that you are a member of C.U.F., if you had been asked to help in the designing of the May Crowning liturgy, what would you have compromised on? What would you have absolutely rejected? Explain your answers.
3. Pretending you are Sr. Peg, how do you feel about the pending meeting with C.U.F.? Can you identify any common ground that would make it possible to include C.U.F. parishioners in liturgy planning?
4. The following Scripture (Galatians 2:4) describes a "spying" activity in first generation Christianity. What encourages such activity? "Certain false claimants to the title of brother were smuggled in; they wormed their way into the group to spy on the freedom we enjoy in Christ Jesus and thereby to make slaves of us...."

Situation Three
"THEY'RE BABY KILLERS!"
(Tom, chairperson of the Christian Service Commission, is conducting a meeting of the commission.)

Mrs. White: Tom, you are a pro-life person, aren't you?

Tom: I hope so. I've purchased a lot of pro-life resources for the parish. At Molly's last teachers' meeting I encouraged all of them to promote life every chance they get.

Mrs. White: Do you belong to S.T.O.R.K.? I do.

Tom: What does "stork" mean?

Mrs. White: Stop The Optional Random Killing.

Tom: Didn't that group have something to do with the bombing of an abortion clinic in the city?

Mrs. White: Yes, we did, and good riddance. The people who work there are baby killers. I think Molly should have S.T.O.R.K. speak to the youth group. Maybe they should speak at Mass, too. It would be better than that woman preacher we had last week.

Tom: What other pro-life issues are you interested in?

Mrs. White: There is only one issue: abortion. God said, "Thou shalt not kill!"

Tom: How do you feel about capital punishment?

Mrs. White: What does that have to do with pro-life? I think all murderers and rapists should be put to death, and maybe even those gang members in the city. I'm afraid to go downtown any more.

Tom: Don't you think that if we are really interested in *life* then maybe we should try to do something about the quality of life in the city that produces those gangs?

Mrs. White: I'm talking about killing babies. Those people in the city live the way they want to. They're the ones having the abortions, too, and with my tax money! At least capital punishment saves on taxes.

Response

1. Describe your immediate feelings upon reading this case. Describe some personal experience that parallels it.

2. Why is it possible for Mrs. White to be so convinced of the absolute evil of abortion and at the same time convinced that capital punishment is good and necessary? (Include in your reflection the influence of politics, culture, and experience on personal moral convictions.)

3. Pretend you are Tom. Using Weber's suggestions for facilitating healing and growth (Chapter 7), do a role play with Mrs. White.

4. Could Mrs. White make a contribution to the parish's pro-life ministry? Explain.

Situation Four
"ALL WE WANTED WERE SOME ANSWERS"
The parish staff at St. Paul is faced with the need to do extensive remodeling of the church building. The previous pastor had deliberately postponed any changes because of his personal resistance to anything new. While pastor, he had frequently spoken publicly against changes being introduced in other parishes of the diocese. Now a small segment of the parish has become very outspoken against initial plans being considered by the parish team and the remodeling committee.

How to deal with this vocal resistance was the topic of this week's team meeting. Sr. Peg brought to the meeting a newspaper article sent to her by a community member in another diocese.

PARISH FACES ULTIMATUM OVER COMMUNION RAIL

Members of St.___Parish in___will have to vote this summer to keep either their parish or the communion rail in their 70-year-old church.

Bishop___of___was preparing ballots which would be used in a parish vote aimed at settling a controversy which began in January when the parish council decided to remove the rail.

The decision will be an agonizing one for the close-knit parish of 110 families.

"It's been a sad state of affairs," parish council member___ said in a phone interview. "Everyone's broken-hearted out here, and we don't know where to turn."

She said 75 percent of the adults in the parish had signed a petition opposing any changes in the interior of the church, which is listed on the National Register of Historic Places.

"The issue," said diocesan spokesman Fr.___, "is not only the communion rail; the issue is the legitimate authority and processes of the church."

The central section of St.___'s ornate marble and brass communion rail was removed on July 3 following approval by the parish council in January.

But on July 4 a group of about 34-40 parishioners met at the church steps to discuss the removal, said____, one of those present.

The parish priest, Rev.____, evidently saw the crowd and feared for his safety. To play it safe, he decided not to confront them, it was observed. Fr.____'s car appeared to be blocked in the parking lot, said Fr.____. He then apparently left through the rectory's back door, walked through a cow pasture, climbed a fence, jumped a creek and got to a road where another priest was waiting in a car, and they drove away.

"All the people wanted were answers, and he took it the wrong way," said another parishioner.

Fr.____, who has since resigned as pastor, could not be reached for comment.

About a dozen parishioners took matters into their own hands by putting the missing section of the rail back in place.

That action prompted a meeting between Bishop____and St.____ parishioners. ____said the bishop told them he was obliged to uphold the authority and processes of the church, and in this case, the parish council's decision.

Bishop____told them they would have to choose between two options: 1) the parish would continue to exist if parishioners would abide by the parish council's decision and remove part of the communion rail, or 2) they could keep the church's interior as it was, but St.____would cease being a parish and the church would become a chapel-museum.

____said the bishop was preparing a ballot which was expected to be ready for the parish by early August.

Response

1. As an outsider looking in, did the situation sometimes strike you as humorous? If so, why was it not humorous to the actual participants? Could it have been?
2. Why are parishioners sensitive about the architecture of their church and its furnishings?

3. Could the harshness and even bitterness that accompanied this struggle have been kept within tolerable limits if factions had been self-critical and had tried to understand the other group? Explain.

4. Choose:

a. Pretend you are the bishop. Explain your decision.

b. Pretend you are a parish council member. Explain your decision.

c. Pretend you belong to the opposing faction. Explain your stand.

Situation Five
"MARY DOESN'T LIKE THAT!"

Fr. Gene usually spends his day off with Fr. Sam, a pastor on the other side of the diocese. When he described the C.U.F. reaction to the parish's May Crowning, Fr. Sam laughed and said, "I can top that! You're lucky to have such an innocent situation. You know what I have to put up with every week?

"About twenty families in the parish believe in the Bayside apparitions. At first we didn't know about it. Then gradually some women showed up in church dressed in blue, from neck to ankles, with a blue beanie covered with a black mantilla. Now there are about twenty. Their daughters dress the same. They—their whole family—always sit in back of church and spend the whole Mass praying out of special prayer books or praying the rosary. They always kneel and seem out of sync with the rest of the congregation. They also kneel to receive communion, and won't receive from a lay eucharistic minister. When I was on vacation the visiting priest had a leg injury and couldn't stand. So there were only lay ministers for communion. One of these Bayside people came to me later to complain that they couldn't go to communion because of that situation. I asked why and found out that during the alleged apparitions Mary had said that her son didn't like any of the changes since Vatican II.

"What's worse is that I have one of these people teaching religion. She was a teacher long before all this happened. She

has a big rosary draped over the Bible on display in her room.
The teachers who share the room keep taking it off the Bible,
but it keeps coming back! She also tells the children that Mary
doesn't like the new religion books."

Response
1. How would you feel if you were in Fr. Sam's situation?
2. Would this situation necessarily weaken the parish community? Explain.
3. If you were Fr. Sam, how would you deal a) with this group's
deviant behavior during Mass, b) with the rosary on the Bible?
4. Why do some parishioners tend to follow visionaries?
5. What elements of a plausibility structure are evident in this
group? (cf. Chapter 4)

Situation Six
THE MYSTERY OF ONE GOD
Fr. Gene described for the parish staff Fr. Sam's predicament
with the Bayside people. This led to a lengthy discussion about
the different beliefs of parishioners today. The staff wondered
how widespread doctrinal pluralism was within their own
parish. Their concern was this: if religious convictions rub off on
the people ministered to, are parish leaders such as themselves
and catechists, for example, the catalysts of even greater diversity and tension in the future? Because the parish catechists
represented a good cross section of the parish, the staff ar-
ranged to interview some of them. The following cases reflect
these private interviews.

John Samson is just short of retirement from his job. He has
been a junior high catechist at St. Paul for about ten years. He
seems very faithful and enthusiastic about his teaching, even
though parents complain regularly that their children do not
like his sessions because they are so boring and he is so strict.
Molly: What is the most important religious truth to you?
John: The mystery of the Blessed Trinity. That is the heart of

our whole religion. If teens today would only take God more seriously, they wouldn't get into so much trouble.

Molly: The mystery of three persons in one God is first in our religious tradition. What got you so interested in this truth?

John: I grew up in a parish called Blessed Trinity. All the time I spent in church—and it was a lot—I would stare at the painting in the sanctuary. It was kind of old-fashioned but I liked it. God the Father was pictured as a severe old man with a long white beard and hair. Just above him was a younger version, obviously Jesus, and above Jesus was a white dove, the Holy Spirit.

Molly: Putting aside for a moment the mystery of Trinity, how do you *feel* about God?

John: I'm kind of uncomfortable with your use of the word "feel." I think religion should be more concerned about what we *know* about God. But anyway...I don't think God is like the fathers I know in the parish. They don't set a good example and are too easy on their kids. Everything goes nowadays. When I was young we were taught that "fear of the Lord" was one of the gifts of the Holy Spirit—or Holy Ghost in those days. No one is afraid of God any more.

Molly: You mean we should be *afraid* of God?

John: Well...sure I do. God is almighty. He can save us or send us to...you know where. That's the way I was taught and you can't teach old dogs new tricks.

Response

1. Is John Samson's attitude toward "fear of God" all that uncommon among parishioners you know? What are some sources of this fear?

2. Using the process of theological reflection (cf. Chapter 7), what kind of God do you (and the group) discover? (One or more of the group might pretend to be John Samson.)

3. In a role play with John Samson, share with him this catechesis from the National Catechetical Directory (NCD), #83-84: God "frees, saves, and loves his people with the love of a father and spouse. His goodness is the source of our eternal hope

and should prompt us to worship him." Can "fear of God" fit
into this catechesis?
4. What parallel to this "fear of God" have you come across in
your ministry?

Situation Seven
THE MYSTERY OF CREATION
Grace and Paul Black team teach one of the fifth grades in the
parish elementary program. This curriculum concerns the sacraments. Grace and Paul have always seemed rather shy parishioners and catechists and so Fr. Gene was never aware of any
particular religious convictions that would interfere with their
teaching. When they got married, Grace left her fundamentalist church and became a Catholic. They now seem upset with
something and Paul is holding a Bible.

Fr. Gene: The parish staff is interviewing a cross section of catechists to discuss informally their faith convictions. This is important because our faith has a way of rubbing off on those we
teach.

Grace: Not only our faith but also what's in the teacher's manu-
al we are using. Do you know what's in the chapter on baptism?
It says that all life in some way has come out of water millions
of years ago and so it's beautiful and natural that water be the
sign of a return to new life.

Paul: That's a sneaky way of talking about evolution and that's
against the Bible and church's teaching.

Grace: Last Saturday my daughter's religion class saw a film-
strip, something about a 15 billion year Advent story. She said
it had a lot about God in it but there were pictures that were a
lot like the ones in their science book in the public school and
that book teaches evolution.

Paul: How can our parish religion program promote evolution
when it says right here in the Bible that God created the world
in seven days?

Fr. Gene: Hold on a minute! I wouldn't say that our religion program promotes any special scientific theory. But wouldn't it be

awful if we shielded our children from scientific knowledge? Science is a gift from God, you know.

Grace: But we can't teach something against the Bible!

Fr. Gene: Didn't the two of you attend my Scripture series? All of the catechists were invited.

Paul: No. We talked to you last year when this same topic came up. But we didn't like how you explained the Book of Genesis.

Fr. Gene: I remember now. Anyway, there is a verse in Scripture that might help you with this matter of evolution. Paul, you have your Bible with you. Would you read out loud chapter 5, verse 7 of John's gospel?

Paul: "But Jesus had an answer for them: 'My Father is at work until now, and I am at work as well.'"

Fr. Gene: If God created everything in seven days, then why does Jesus talk about the Father and himself still working?

Response

1. How might Grace's religious background influence her convictions about creation and evolution? Why would Paul have the same concerns?

2. If you were Fr. Gene, what common religious ground could you share with Grace and Paul? (Note: NCD 85/86 presents a catechesis on creation but does not discuss theories of evolution. Is this absence compatible with the church's role as teacher?)

3. Reflect upon the following statement by Bishop Kenneth Povish of Lansing, Michigan. Do you think it would benefit Grace and Paul?

CREATIONISM RUCKUS

The ruckus in Arkansas over the teaching of "creationism" could well be transplanted to our state. A bill requiring such teaching here only needs to get out of legislative committee. There is something wrongheaded about this controversy that ought to be exposed right from the start. It does no honor to God or to the Scriptures to attribute to the latter more than is in them.

[Bible literalists] want the Book of Genesis to get equal time with Charles Darwin's theories in high school science classes. This is folly.

It presumes that the Bible is a science book, at least a primitive one. The Bible is a collection of religious books. As literature, these books include several different styles of writing, all the way from poetry and prophetic teaching to census lists and historical accounts of events.

The Book of Genesis was never intended to be taken as a scientific description of creation. To say that it was is to a high degree unscriptural and untheological. What the Book of Genesis teaches about the universe is that the God of the Bible is responsible for its existence and that it is good.

I agree that the Bible ought to be taught in the public schools of the land, preferably in religion classes. If that's not feasible, then in literature classes. But there is no justification for its use in classes of science strictly so-called.

Bishop Kenneth J. Povish
Lansing Catholic Weekly

Situation Eight
THE MYSTERY OF JESUS
Molly met for coffee with Jean, a very popular senior high catechist and Molly's close friend. They grew up together in St. Paul parish. Jean went on to the state university. While there she became involved in the Jesus movement of the late 1960s and was rebaptized in a river with hundreds of other university students. During those years Molly had a hard time understanding Jean's new way of talking about Jesus, as if nothing else in religion, or in the world for that matter, was important. And nothing she talked about had any connection to their earlier religious formation. Jean even implied at times that she was worried about Molly's salvation. In recent years Jean seems to have done a complete turn-around.

Molly: Jean, what is the center of your faith? What religious truth do you rally around?

Jean: Right now I don't know. You know my history. My "Jesus thing" at the university didn't last. Now I think it was just an angry rejection of all that old-fashioned stuff we were taught here at St. Paul; you know, the baby Jesus and the bloody death on the cross. Most of all, I was angry that we weren't taught or rather weren't convinced that all we had to do was submit totally to Jesus' saving power. If you remember, the Miraculous Medal was pushed on us as much as if not more than, Jesus' saving power.

Molly: So, where are you now, religiously? You said a moment ago that you don't know. You seem to be popular with the teens.

Jean: Maybe I'm popular because I'm willing to search with them instead of laying something heavy and definite on them. To tell the truth, I don't think I believe in Jesus any more. If he had been born in the Orient he would be called Buddha. If he had been born a woman in our own time he or rather she would be Mother Theresa. There are days when I think that Christianity is just a great big accident of history. It probably would have been wiped out and lost in history if it hadn't joined forces with the powerful Roman Empire!

Molly: Is this what you are teaching in your religion class?

Jean: In a way, yes. But not that last thing I said about Christianity being an accident of history. That's my own feeling right now. I try to get the teens to search for the *meaning* of Jesus in their life. I want them to avoid both mistakes I made: swallowing everything religious I was taught as a child and then swallowing a bunch of new stuff while at the university. It wasn't until recently that I started really searching. I don't have many answers yet and I won't teach what I don't believe or haven't personally experienced.

Molly: So, right now you can't say if you believe that Jesus is God?

Jean: That's right.

Response
1. Chart the changes in Jean's faith in Jesus Christ beginning in grade school. What influenced these changes?
2. In what ways is Jean's journey of faith different from or similar to your own and your friends'?
3. May Jean's crisis of faith be damaging to the faith of those she teaches? Explain.
4. If a delegation of parishioners requested the dismissal of Jean from teaching religion, how would you react?

Situation Nine
THE MYSTERY OF THE SPIRIT
Sr. Peg's first interview is with Dave Smith, a member of the confirmation team and a parishioner with whom she happens to be very uncomfortable. For a while he was the leader of the ecumenical prayer group which Sr. Peg occasionally attends. Recently Dave seems to be more active in other groups around the city, especially businessmen's prayer breakfasts. He prides himself on his gift of healing and has at times turned his weekly confirmation preparation session into healing sessions centered around teen involvement with drugs, alcohol, and premarital sex. The parish staff found out about this when a delegation of parents complained about the confirmation preparation program.
Sr. Peg: Dave, I know you're a charismatic. How did it happen?
Dave: It's a wonderful story the way the Lord led me to a new way of Christian living. You may not know, but at one time I was an alcoholic. One day my wife threw me out of the house. Walking away I looked back and there was a white dove hovering over the house. Then it flew before me, leading me. At the time I didn't know if it was leading me away from something or to something. It seemed to stop over that Church of God on Second Avenue. I went in and talked to the pastor. When I told him I was a Catholic, he suggested I see Mrs. Green at my own parish, St. Paul. I did. Went to a prayer meeting. About a month later I was baptized in the Spirit. I haven't touched a drop since.

Sr. Peg: Dave, the parish staff is upset that you have been conducting healing services in your confirmation class without our knowledge or permission.

Dave: A gift of the Spirit is much more powerful than your permission. The Spirit has asked me to heal others and I do so on a regular basis at other groups around the city. I figure that if I can heal these teens now they won't have to suffer like I did.

Sr. Peg: The parents feel that if their children have a problem they should get some professional help and not some miraculous healing.

Dave: Professional help isn't necessary if you pray and have faith.

Sr. Peg: Didn't the apostle Paul say the gifts of the Spirit should be used for the good of the community? Is what you are doing, without informing the parents or parish staff, good for St. Paul parish?

Dave: I'm sorry you feel this way. That's why I have invited teens from my group to come to my house. I've done this only after praying. I don't feel that the parish confirmation program is doing what it should. Maybe I should just resign from the confirmation team.

Response

1. Describe your feelings as you read this case. Could you work with Dave Smith in parish ministry? Explain.
2. What meaning of the mystery of "Spirit," common in church teaching, might Sr. Peg and Dave Smith agree on? What seems to lie at the source of the tension between them?
3. How do Sr. Peg and Dave Smith differ in their understanding of what "parish" is?
4. Would you be glad to accept Dave's resignation from the confirmation team? Explain.

Situation Ten

THE MYSTERY OF CHURCH

Tom had been expecting Helen Grey, a third-grade catechist and a member of the Christian Service Commission, but her husband, Gene, showed up instead.

Tom: Gene, I was expecting Helen.

Gene: I know. I told her to stay home so that I could talk with you. I asked her to quit teaching and her other volunteer work in the parish.

Tom: Why would you do that? She has been a wonderful catechist. Molly says the children just love her. And the Christian Service Commission would really miss her.

Gene: That might be true. But I don't want her to be giving any more time to the church until it stops causing so much scandal.

Tom: What do you mean? You seem to be uneasy about something.

Gene: I'm sick and tired of what the church is turning into. We're supposed to be united to Rome, but I see stuff going on that Rome doesn't approve of.

Tom: Could you give me some examples?

Gene: Well, for one thing, Molly sent all the teachers a notice of a day of fasting and prayer over at St. Gregory's, for nuclear disarmament. Our churches were built to give glory to the supernatural. Now they are shamelessly used to promote political issues. The Holy Father doesn't want us in politics. And it's a scandal to the people.

Tom: Gene, I think you're mixing a lot of stuff together that needs to be explained in pieces. For example, Pope John Paul himself preaches peace. And the church's restriction on political involvement had to do with priests holding elected office.

Gene: I figured you'd have some fancy explanation. The fact of the matter is that priests and religious—even those who used to be good nuns—are taking part in political lobbying and illegal demonstration. What happened to the church teaching about obeying the law, that giving to Caesar what belongs to Caesar thing? Did you see that list of speakers over at St. Gregory's? It looked like a "Who's Who" of all the radicals. That day of fasting and prayer was more political than spiritual. No wonder some people think the church should pay taxes.

Tom: Gene, it is very difficult to talk with you. You seem so closed minded about what the church should be. The church's mission is to proclaim the gospel and the heart of the gospel is love. In fact you could say that the heart of the gospel is peace. Jesus said: "Blessed are the peacemakers."

Gene: There weren't any Russians around when Jesus said that! The Holy Father has pointed out that peace talk is often a cover up for sinister forces that could lead to the false peace of totalitarian regimes.

Tom: What have you been reading...or who have you been talking to? It surely hasn't been Helen, your wife. She is so devoted to the church and the mission of the church.

Gene: She's not going to spend any more time for the church until the church becomes what it should be!

Response

1. Choose one issue in this case to reflect upon, one which you consider to be a core issue.

2. How is it possible for Helen and Gene Grey, as a married couple, to have such divergent convictions about what "church" should be and do?

3. List some related issues to your choice of the core issue. Which do you think could be resolved? Not resolved?

4. Review #96 of the NCD along with 155-159. What influence might politics, culture, and experience have on Gene's personal convictions about what "church" should be?

Situation Eleven
THE MYSTERY OF SACRAMENTS
Molly and Sr. Peg are meeting with parents whose children will receive either first communion or first reconciliation this year. The parish policies regarding these two sacraments were developed under the leadership of the present team. They reflect the evolving policies of the diocese. The primary responsibility of preparing the children lies with the parents. The sacraments are received individually when the parents consid-

er their child ready. Special first communion "costumes" are frowned upon by the team but tolerated. Catechesis for reconcil- iation begins in grade four and the sacrament is celebrated in a communal fashion by the children.

Molly's introduction to the parent meeting covered the gen- eral area of the sacramental dimension of all of reality, that everything in human life can become a sign pointing to God's wonderful presence and saving power. She emphasized that if parents set an example for their children by way of an active appreciation of all the signs and wonders in life, the children would be well prepared for the celebration of the sacraments in church.

First parent: By the time the children get to the fifth grade, they couldn't care less about sacraments.

Second parent: By that time, all they're interested in is talking about boy friends and girl friends.

Molly: (to second parent) But that's normal. Even these begin- ning signs of friendship can be tied in with the whole notion of sacraments.

Second parent: I don't see the connection. The sacraments are too important to put on the level of their boy-girl stuff.

Third parent: I think the children lose their interest in the sac- raments because we don't make them special any more. We didn't have this problem when there was group first communion and they all dressed special. Now they go just any Sunday they want to, dressed the way they want to. It's not going to be some- thing they'll remember all their life the way ours was.

Sr. Peg: Our parish guidelines for the sacraments were devel- oped with a lot of thought. We felt that the emphasis on spe- cial communion clothes interfered with what is more impor- tant: the mystery of the moment and the meaning of the sacrament. When we think back to our first communion, don't we remember the externals more than the meaning of what was happening?

First parent: If the old way is okay in the other parishes, why isn't it okay for our parish?

Second parent: I think the parents should be allowed to vote on how they want first communion to take place.

Response

1. Pretend you are Molly or St. Peg. What emotions do you feel as the parents begin to question your sacrament policies? What are the sources of your feelings?

2. Would you allow parents to vote on parish sacrament policies? Explain.

3. How does the parents' preoccupation with clothes and scheduling of sacraments fit into the church's catechesis? (NCD #97, 114-126). Why might it be understandable that parents are preoccupied with what staff considers non-essentials?

4. Prepare a role play of one of your own experiences related to the theme of this case.

Situation Twelve
THE LIFE OF GRACE

Bob is a catechist for grade seven. He is a very faithful parishioner and goes pretty much by the book in teaching.

Molly: Bob, what is the most important religious truth for you? What gives your faith a solid base?

Bob: That's an easy question, the fact that Jesus died for us and took away our sins.

Molly: That is a pretty important truth. Does it influence your teaching very much?

Bob: No, but I wish it would. Those kids in my class couldn't care less about sin or salvation. Last week I asked how many went to church the previous Sunday. I counted at least a third of the class who didn't go.

Molly: If the parents don't go, the children can hardly be responsible.

Bob: That's the same excuse they gave me. And yet not a single one of them has gone to confession for almost a year. I asked them that, too. And they all went to communion at our junior high liturgy last week.

Molly: You said that your most important religious conviction is that Jesus died for us and took away our sins. How do you think Jesus would feel about the young people in your group?

Bob: I don't think he would be very happy. He commanded us to go to church on Sunday. If these young people nowadays want to believe, they have to meet Jesus half-way. So, the least they could do is go to church. And if they don't, the least they could do is go to confession. I think most of the problem comes from the changes you and Fr. Gene made about confession. Children don't have to go to confession any more before first communion. So they don't learn it at the right time. And the rumor is that the remodeling in church is going to remove the confessionals and we're going to have a room where we have to confess face to face with Fr. Gene. Do you think young people will ever do that?

Response
1. If you were Molly, how would you feel hearing Bob say: "If these young people nowadays want to believe, they have to meet Jesus halfway. So, the least they could do is go to confession"?
2. What might be the sources of Bob's convictions?
3. How do these convictions match the church's catechesis? (NCD #98-100, 124)
4. What common ground about the attitude of Jesus toward sinners might Molly and Bob work toward? Suggest some Scripture sources.

Situation Thirteen
THE MORAL LIFE
Sheila is a confirmation catechist. She is active in the peace and justice movement and has been effective in involving the teens in service activities.

Sheila: Tom, I've got a real problem. Some of the Catholics I know think I did something terrible in breaking the civil law at our last peace demonstration. They said it was a sin and that I was setting a bad example for the young people in the confirmation program.

Tom: People kind of lump all laws together, God's laws and human laws.

Sheila: But they aren't aware of the terrible sin in their life. They don't care about the evils of the stockpiling of nuclear weapons. At the ballot box they vote for politicians who have a record of voting against aid to the homeless in the cities—but for aid for dictators in Latin America.

Tom: Sheila, not everybody has your convictions.

Sheila: You can say that again. The other week in class we discussed the difference in what parents think is a sin and what the teens think is a sin. Right on top of the list for parents was "not going to church."

Tom: What was on the top of the teens' list?

Sheila: Well, actually they had a hard time making a list at first. Then they came up with "putting your friends down." But eventually they came up with some more things like "showing off" and "not caring about people who are starving."

Tom: Why do you think the lists of sins from parents and the teens are so different?

Response

1. What do you feel is the core issue in this case? Related issues?

2. Reflect on some reasons why many Catholics come down hard on civil disobedience as practiced by other Catholics and especially church leaders. Can you understand their feelings?

3. Can you justify Sheila's approach toward morality on the basis of NCD #101-105?

4. "Why do you think the lists of sins from parents and the teens are so different?"

Situation Fourteen

THE MYSTERY OF SAINTS

Josie is the mother of one of about twelve Hispanic families in St. Paul parish. Her own parents were migrant field workers who had settled in the parish almost a generation ago.

Molly: Josie, what is your favorite part of the Catholic religion?

Josie: Well, what has excited me ever since I was a little girl is devotion to the saints. I know that this isn't very popular any more.

Molly: But devotion to the saints has always been part of our Catholic tradition.

Josie: I know. But it's embarrassing sometimes. I've had people tell me that Jesus is enough. I shouldn't feel that I have to pray to the saints. In fact, I have something embarrassing to ask you. My grandpa is visiting us from New Mexico. He's about eighty years old. He wants me to find out if Fr. Gene will make him some St. Ignatius water.

Molly: St. Ignatius water? I never heard of that.

Josie: Well, it's something like holy water. Grandpa has always used it to rub on the sores on his legs.

Molly: I think Fr. Gene would be glad to help your grandpa. How does a person go about making St. Ignatius water?

Josie: Grandpa told me to tell Fr. Gene that he would bring everything Fr. Gene would need. He has a specially blessed medal of St. Ignatius and some kind of prayer card in what looks like Latin. At least it's not Spanish. All Fr. Gene has to do is to dip the medal into a jug of water while saying the special prayers. Sounds crazy doesn't it? But grandpa says it works!

Response
1. Can you justify the church's tradition of honoring saints and praying to them. If so, can you justify the church's reform of these traditions?
2. Would you be comfortable or uncomfortable with Josie's request? Explain.
3. Do you feel that the St. Ignatius water actually does help Josie's grandpa's legs?
4. If you were Fr. Gene, would you make the St. Ignatius water? Explain.

Situation Fifteen
THE MYSTERY OF THE LAST THINGS

Fr. Gene has just finished a lengthy session with a family making arrangements for a funeral. Several members of the family regularly attend a Tridentine Mass on the other side of the city. Their first request was that their Tridentine priest "say" the funeral Mass. If this wasn't possible, then they insisted that Fr. Gene at least wear black vestments for the funeral and not put "that white thing" over the expensive coffin they picked out. And they didn't want anything at the funeral home except the rosary. They would return later to confirm all details.

Fr. Gene has gone from that session to an interview with Mary who has been teaching religion ever since the parish began. She is almost eighty years old, teaches third grade, and is able to weave together the traditional and the contemporary in her classroom.

Fr. Gene: (after telling Mary what had just occurred in his office) I bet you have had to do a lot of rethinking about your faith the past twenty years, with all the changes in the Catholic church.

Mary: You can say that again. But it's all for the better. When I go, and it won't be long at my age, I want Sr. Peg to coordinate some children to do a liturgical dance around my coffin. People today have forgotten how scary the old religion could be. Let me tell you a story about what happened when I was about twelve years old. We had one of those parish missions which used to be popular, kind of like a week retreat. Well, one morning the priest talked to us children as part of our school day. He didn't just scare us with stuff about the consequences of mortal sin, eternal hell fire and all that. He told us that the end of the world was right around the corner. He read to us some prophecies from some saint about the end of the world.

Well, that night when the sun went down the sky had the funniest color, and the sun was big and red like it was going to explode. And I thought to myself: "This is it! The world is going to end tonight and I'm going to hell!" You know, in those days it was easy to think you were in mortal sin the way we were taught.

Well, anyway, that night I dreamed that the world did end. There was a judgment. Strangely, how a person fared in judgment depended on what size cookie they were holding. Anyway, almost no people got to heaven. One of my sisters was one of the lucky ones. Almost everybody was in purgatory or hell. And below hell, mind you, was a worse place called limbo with only a few people there and one of them was my brother. I woke up, sweating, fell back to sleep and dreamed it all over again. But the second time I got to heaven!

It wasn't until recent years that I began to relax about death and what would be waiting for me. That bad sermon of long ago stuck with me and spoiled a lot of my life.

Response
1. Pretending you are Fr. Gene, what emotions do you experience as the family insists on traditionalist features for the funeral?
2. Still pretending you are Fr. Gene, what compromises would you consider? What would you stand firm on? Give reasons for your decisions.
3. What do you feel lies at the source of a traditionalist's convictions? Do you think a traditionalist would agree with you about your answer?
4. Why would Mary, who came out of the same background as these traditionalists, have such a different attitude?
5. In general, do you feel that parishioners have a mature attitude toward the mystery of death and what comes afterwards?

CONCLUSION

Catholic parishes are alive and healthy. Large crowds still gather for parish liturgies, worshipping with a fair amount of enthusiasm. New ministers, both women and men, are in the sanctuary. Parishioners and visitors are met at the church door by cheerful greeters. New parish structures are in place and working: parish councils, commissions, and ad hoc committees. Evangelization efforts, such as the adult catechumenate, are beginning to take hold. Renewal movements awaken new interest in Scripture and in community building in small groups. Parishioners hear the gospel and respond, sometimes with great personal sacrifice, with efforts toward peace, justice, and human rights. Parish programs, staffed by volunteers, reach out to the poor, the hungry, the handicapped, the lonely, and the broken. Creative ministries abound. Volunteers still fill the ranks of catechists. Lay eucharistic ministers share the parish's holy bread with the sick and shut-ins. Lay parishioners sign up for comprehensive ministry training. And charismatics spread joy, spirit, and healing.

This variety within the parish, signs of life and health, may also become the cause of stress and conflict. On the darkest day, a particular parish may seem to be crumbling to pieces or at least working against itself. Parishioners seem to be committed to contradictory religious beliefs or at least to different priorities and themes. They seem to practice their faith independently of other parishioners and contrary to themes promoted by parish leaders. Factions compete for attention or for some level of power and influence. The parish staff, and parish leaders on all levels, at times feel under siege.

This situation is not necessarily destructive of unity or of the parish community's health. It must be considered in the context of a church that has experienced pluralism of practical faith as a norm, without losing its fundamental unity, throughout most of its 2000 years.

There is evidence that this diversity of priorities and religious practice will continue in the church. The probability is that it will increase. Human society and culture form the real environment of the parish. Trends within this environment will echo in the parish: freedom of thought and expression, questioning of authority, championing of current causes, etc. The parish is also part of the larger diocesan, national, and universal church. Tensions within this broader church will be reflected in the local church, the parish.

Pluralism of religious convictions and practices cannot be wished away, prayed away, nor ministered away. Parish leaders, who grew up with a strong Catholic identity in a smoothly functioning parish before the 1960s may prefer the stability of yesterday, even though they subscribe to today's freedom of thought and expression. There is little choice but to accept the challenge of coordinating a plurality of religious convictions and practices into an experience of catholicity. The challenge becomes, then, not how to eradicate pluralism but how to put it into context, how to live with it, how to minister in the midst of it, and, in the best of times, how to celebrate it.

Efforts toward a renewal of Catholic identity among parishioners are crucial if this challenge is to be met. Catholic identity is not primarily an individual or isolated experience: "Who am *I*?" It is, rather, a community experience: "Who are *we*?" This shared Catholic identity was lost, through no one's fault, during changes and shifts in both church and society over the past twenty years. Themes were rearranged, priorities upset, and structures of faith remodeled. A renewal of Catholic identity does not mean, however, the restoring of former religious practices, attitudes, and even beliefs upon which the former identity was founded. It means, instead, a rediscovery of and celebration of community among parishioners who live their faith with different emphases and themes.

Restoring this community experience or Catholic identity is a wholesome and holy ministry. It is a ministry of patience, understanding, compromise, and the primary virtue of love. It is a ministry of assertiveness, clarity of speech and hearing, honest theological reflection, and reconciliation. It is a ministry of public relations and conflict resolution.

A community experience of Catholic identity will tolerate a great variety of religious beliefs and practices. This does not mean, however, that all are on equal footing. There is a hierarchy in religious practice just as there is a hierarchy in religious truths. A catholic religious identity expresses, first of all, the core teachings of the church, most of which are shared by other Christian churches. It also expresses those religious beliefs and practices peculiar to Catholic tradition. Among these are an emphasis on sacraments, primacy of the eucharist, appreciation of ritual, devotion to saints and especially to Mary, and a sense of church that includes a bond with other parishes, dioceses, and with the bishop of Rome, who ministers to the whole church with a special gift.

A community experience of Catholic identity will be sensitive to current themes promoted by, or in some cases, agonized over, by church leaders and laity alike: peace, poverty, economy, life issues, human rights, role of the laity and especially of women. It is here that a plurality of conviction and practice can happen without threatening the more fundamental Catholic identity centered in core religious truths and Catholic tradition.

A community experience of Catholic identity will be tolerant also of parishioners' involvement in religious movements broader than the ministry and membership of a particular parish: charismatic renewal, marriage encounter, etc. It is here, also, that a plurality of opinion and practice can exist without threatening the more fundamental identity.

Finally, a community experience of Catholic identity will be conscious of the validity of diversity, united in Christ, and sensitive to his words (John 15: 11-12; 17-21):

All this I tell you that my joy may be complete. This is my commandment: love one another as I have loved you...that all may be one as you, Father, are in me, and I in you; I pray that they may be one in us, that the world may believe that you sent me.

NOTES

CHAPTER 1

1. See Edward K. Braxton, "What Happened?" in *The Wisdom Community* (New York: Paulist Press, 1980), pp. 17-50.
2. Andrew Greeley, "The Emergence of the Communal Catholic," *The Communal Catholic: A Personal Manifesto* (New York: The Seabury Press, 1976), pp. 1-17.
3. Karl Rahner, *The Shape of the Church to Come* (New York: Crossroad, 1983), pp. 23-24.
4. Peter L. Berger, *The Heretical Imperative* (Garden City, New York: Doubleday, 1979), pp. 26-28.
5. Rahner, *Church*, p. 38.
6. See *Notre Dame Study of Catholic Parish Life*, Report #10, "Parish as Community" (Notre Dame, Indiana: Memorial Library).

CHAPTER 2

1. Avery Dulles, S.J., *Models of the Church* (Garden City, New York: Doubleday, 1978).
2. Raymond E. Brown and John P. Meier, *Antioch & Rome* (Ramsey, New Jersey: Paulist Press, 1983), p. vii.
3. *A Message to the People of God and the Final Report*, Extraordinary Synod of Bishops, Rome, 1985 (Washington, D.C.: United States Catholic Conference, 1986), p. 18.
4. Evelyn Eaton and James D. Whitehead, *Community of Faith: Models and Strategies for Developing Christian Communities* (New York: The Seabury Press, 1982), p. 9.
5. Raymond E. Brown, *The Churches the Apostles Left Behind* (New York: Paulist Press, 1984), cf. any chapter.

CHAPTER 3

1. Raymond E. Brown, *The Community of the Beloved Disciple: The Lives, Loves, and Hates of an Individual Church in New Testament Times* (New York: Paulist Press, 1979), pp. 114-123.
2. Will Durant, *The Story of Civilization*. Vol. IV: *The Age of Faith* (New York: Simon & Schuster, 1950), p. 8.
3. Durant, *Faith*, pp. 771-776. For insight into how these here-

sies functioned in the thirteenth and fourteenth centuries, read Umberto Eco's popular thriller and Gothic novel, *The Name of the Rose* (New York: Harcourt, Brace, Jovanovich, 1983).

4. For an historical overview of spirituality over nineteen centuries, see Richard McBrien, *Catholicism* (Minneapolis: Winston Press, 1981), Chapter XXVIII.

5. Josef A. Jungmann, S.J., *Public Worship: A Survey* (Collegeville, Minnesota: The Liturgical Press, 1957), p. 56.

CHAPTER 4

1. The term "conventional" describes the overall expression of Catholic faith as it functioned in Catholic parishes during the generations prior to Vatican II.

2. Peter L. Berger, *Facing Up to Modernity* (New York: Basic Books, Inc., 1977), p. 173.

3. Edward K. Braxton, *The Wisdom Community* (New York: Paulist Press, 1980), p. 20. Note: A shared common meaning is the result of a process of knowing that sociologists call "objectivation." What was subjectively experienced by others perhaps long ago is objectified by way of language, customs, and rituals. The experiences of old can be experienced again by repeating a ritual. Most of religious reality, for example what it meant to be Catholic in the pre-Vatican II era, had been socially constructed in this way over a period of many centuries. See. Peter L. Berger and Thomas Luckmann, *The Social Construction of Reality* (Garden City, New York: Doubleday, 1966), pp. 35ff, 60ff.

4. Franz Jozef van Beeck, S.J., *Catholic Identity After Vatican II* (Chicago: Loyola University Press, 1985), p. 4.

5. Raymond E. Brown, *The Community of the Beloved Disciple: The Life, Loves, and Hates of an Individual Church in New Testament Times* (New York: Paulist Press, 1979), p. 14ff.

6. Peter L. Berger, *Rumor of Angels* (Garden City, New York: Doubleday, 1969), p. 23.

7. Berger, *Rumor*, p. 22.

8. Berger, *Rumor*, pp. 45ff.

CHAPTER 5

1. Edward K. Braxton, *The Wisdom Community* (New York: Paulist Press, 1980), pp. 40-41.

2. John Powell, S.J., *A Reason to Live! A Reason to Die!* (Niles,

Illinois: Argus Communications, 1972), p. 15.
3. Franz Josef van Beek, *Catholic Identity After Vatican II* (Chicago: Loyola University Press, 1985), p. 4ff.
4. See Gloria Durka and Joanmarie Smith, *Modeling God: Religious Education for Tomorrow* (New York: Paulist Press, 1976).
5. van Beek, *Identity*, p. 8.
6. Rosemary Haughton, *The Passionate God* (New York: Paulist Press, 1981), p. 3.
7. Haughton, *God*, p. 3.
8. Kathleen R. Fischer, *The Inner Rainbow: The Imagination in Christian Life* (New York: Paulist Press, 1983), p. 1.
9. *National Catholic Reporter*, October 2, 1987 (VOL. 23, No. 43).

CHAPTER 6
1. *Sharing the Light of Faith: National Catechetical Directory for Catholics of the United States* (Washington, D.C.: United States Catholic Conference, 1979), 24.
2. NCD, 47.
3. *General Catechetical Directory* (Washington, D.C.: United States Catholic Conference, 1971), 43.
4. NCD, 47.

CHAPTER 7
1. John R. Zaums, "Rebuilding Our Pluralistic Parishes: The Adult Educator's Challenge," in *Christian Adulthood: A Catechetical Resource* (Washington, D.C.: United States Catholic Conference, 1984), p. 78.
2. For a further discussion on the tolerance of views in practical church administration, see Chapter 13, "A New Consensus of the Middle: Is It Possible?" Richard G. Hutchenson, Jr., *Mainline Churches and the Evangelicals: A Challenging Crisis?* (Atlanta: John Knox Press, 1981).
3. Karl Rahner, *The Shape of the Church to Come* (New York: Crossroads, 1983), p. 36.
4. Rahner, *Church*, p. 36.
5. Rahner, *Church*, p. 37.
6. Jacques Weber, S.J., "The Problem of Catholic Fundamentalism," in *Christian Adulthood: A Cathetical Resource* (Washington, D.C.: United States Catholic Conference, 1984), p. 83.

7. For a comprehensive introduction to theological reflection, see James D. and Evelyn Eaton Whitehead, *Method in Ministry: Theological Reflection and Christian Ministry* (New York: The Seabury Press, 1983), cf. Part One.

8. For this particular model of theological reflection the author expresses appreciation to Paulist Leadership and Renewal Project, 5 Park Street, Boston, Massachusetts, 02108, "Process-Model for Consensus-Building," 1983,

9. "Ritual speaking" has been coined to describe talking about religious matters or religious experience. Another term might be "God-talk." It is an example of "objectivation" (cf. footnote #3, Chapter Four). It is also an example of "conversational network" discussed in Chapter Four.

10. Marla J. Selvidge, ed., *Fundamentalism Today: What Makes It So Attractive!* (Elgin, Illinois: Brethren Press, 1984), p. 25.

11. Avery Dulles, S.J., "The Symbolic Structure of Revelation," in *Theological Studies* 41 (1980): 57.

CHAPTER 8

1. An obvious difficulty in using the tradition of the church in any dialogue are the different ways Scripture, theology, and official and unofficial teaching are approached by parish ministers and parishioners. Cf. Chapter 7, section "Theological Reflection."

2. The following is an example of specialized resources related to just one issue facing the church and the local parish: the issue of women's role within the church. For this bibliography the author is grateful to Sr. Dena M. Baronn, associate pastor, St. John Vianney Church, Diocese of Saginaw, Michigan:

Ashe, Kay. *Today's Woman Tomorrow's Church*. Chicago: The Thomas More Press, 1983.

Cunningham, S.S.C.M. *The Role of Women in Eccesial Ministry: Biblical and Patristic Foundations*. Washington, D.C.: United States Catholic Conference, 1976.

Foley, Nadine, O.P., ed. *Preaching and the Non-Ordained*. Collegeville, Minnesota: The Liturgical Press, 1983.

Gryson, Roger. *The Ministry of Women in the Early Church*. Collegeville, Minnesota: The Liturgical Press, 1976.

Cunningham, Agnes, SSCM; Susanne Breckel, RSM; *et al*, *Women in Ministry: A Sisters' View*. Chicago: NAWR Publications, 1972.

Hewitt, Emily C. and Hiatt, Suzanne R. *Women Priests: Yes or No?* New York: The Seabury Press, 1973.

Prokes, Sister M. Timothy SSND. *Women's Challenge: Ministry in the Flesh*. Denville, New Jersey: Dimension Books, 1977.

Stagg, Evelyn and Frank. *Woman in the World of Jesus*. Philadelphia: The Westminster Press, 1978.

Stendahl, Krister. *The Bible and the Role of Women*. Philadelphia: Fortress Press, 1966.

Schüssler-Fiorenza, Elisabeth. *Bread Not Stone: The Challenge of Feminist Biblical Interpretation*. Boston: Beacon Press, 1984.

Swidler, Leonard. *Biblical Affirmations of Women*. Philadelphia: The Westminster Press, 1979.

Tetlow, Elisabeth, M. *Women and Ministry in the New Testament*. New York: Paulist Press, 1980.

Theological Studies. entire issue. Vol. 36, No. 4. December, 1975.

Wahlberg, Rachel Conrad. *Jesus and the Freed Woman*. New York: Paulist Press, 1978.

See also Lavinia Byrne's *Women Before God*. Mystic, Connecticut: Twenty-Third Publications, 1988.

3. Eric Berne, M.D., *Transactional Analysis in Psychotherapy* (New York: Grove Press, Inc., 1961). See also the Introduction and Part I of Berne's *Games People Play* (New York: Grove Press, Inc., 1964), and *I'm OK—You're OK* by Thomas A. Harris, M.D. (New York: Harper & Row, 1973).